OUT OF CONTEXT
A Creative Approach to Strategic Management

General Editor

CYNTHIA WAGNER WEICK, PH.D.

THOMSON

SOUTH-WESTERN

Australia · Canada · Mexico · Singapore · Spain · United Kingdom · United States

THOMSON
™
SOUTH-WESTERN

Out of Context: A Creative Approach to Strategic Management
Cynthia Wagner Weick

VP/Editorial Director:
Jack W. Calhoun

VP/Editor-in-Chief:
Michael P. Roche

Acquisitions Editor:
Joe Sabatino

Developmental Editors:
Molly Flynn
Judith O'Neill

Marketing Manager:
Jacquelyn Carrillo

Production Editor:
Heather Mann

Manufacturing Coordinator:
Rhonda Utley

Technology Project Editor:
Kristen Meere

Media Editor:
Karen L. Schaffer

Design Project Manager:
Rik Moore

Production House:
Argosy Publishing

Cover Designer:
JWR Design Interaction, LLC

Cover Images:
© Digital Vision

Printer:
Webcom Limited
Toronto, Ontario

To glw, rw, and blw

CONTENTS

Strategic management is, arguably, among the most challenging of business courses to teach. As the capstone course in many business schools, it is highly interdisciplinary and requires integration of all conceptual and operational levels of management. Students, who often have little if any direct experience with the upper levels of an organization, must show a command of the processes that company leaders use to conceive and communicate long-term goals and orchestrate the means to reach them. Regardless of individual interests or proclivities, students must quickly learn how the various functional areas that comprise a business work together to implement strategy.

Success in strategic management requires not only strong analytical skills but also the ability to think conceptually and creatively. It is both science and art. As early as the 1950s, R. L. Katz argued that corporate executives needed a variety of skills, which he arranged in a three-tiered pyramid (Katz, 1954). At the base of the pyramid, Katz placed technical skills; in the middle, human skills; and at the top, conceptual skills. More recently, in "The Fall and Rise of Strategic Planning" (1994), Henry Mintzberg distinguished between analytical and synthetic approaches to strategic management and noted that organizations benefit from each. To Mintzberg, however, "real strategic change requires not merely rearranging the established categories," through analytically-based formal planning, "but inventing new ones."

How, then, do we learn to invent new categories, and to conceptualize as well as to analyze? Skills in creative thinking are not readily developed by relying only on materials currently available to strategic management instructors. Textbooks and the tools that augment them, most notably the case method and computer-based simulations, are highly valuable in developing analytically-based problem-solving skills. However, cases do not routinely stretch students' thinking much beyond the scenario they present; and simulations are similarly restrictive, limiting decision making to possibilities programmed into the underlying software.

Out of Context: A Creative Approach to Strategic Management cultivates creative thinking in business strategy courses by using metaphor to explore the unfamiliar. In this sense, metaphor is more than a poetic embellishment, but a means to uncover new ways of envisioning the future. The articles in this collection provide insights into strategy from a wide variety of non-business realms: athletics, military strategy, philosophy, science, and art. Not intended to substitute for traditional texts, cases, and simulations, *Out of Context* instead augments these resources with an additional creative tool. Consequently, students leave the course with a rich and complex set of skills—both analytical and synthetic—for thinking strategically.

The idea of using metaphor in business is not original. Related literature is scattered throughout academic, trade, and popular books and journals; and a cottage industry of consultancies that use metaphor in organizational development has emerged. Casting a wider net shows that preoccupation with metaphor goes back at least as far as Aristotle, and metaphor has been fodder for more modern philosophical and linguistic treatises such as those by George Lakoff and Mark Johnson (1980). However, several years ago, when I began to see the value of incorporating metaphor into my strategic management courses, I found a gap in the available literature. Books that focus on a single metaphorical context are available, as are books that address multiple metaphors through the eyes of a single author. But no source existed that brought together a variety of authors who use comparisons from non-business contexts to enlighten and enliven our understanding of strategic management. The result, *Out of Context,* draws from diverse realms and authors. Not only does the collection appeal to a wide audience, it makes evident the rich and often less obvious range of metaphors that are of value to strategy.

The collection is intended to provide an intellectually challenging journey: one that makes the reader *think*. With hope, it will demonstrate that poetic license offers a unique manner of ensuring that business students and practitioners cultivate the creativity that success in strategic management demands.

INSTRUCTIONAL SUPPORT

Online support is available on the text's dedicated web site at *http://wagner-weick.swlearning.com/*. An Instructor's Manual, constructed to accompany this text, is available for download to qualified faculty, with answers to end-of-section questions, assignment ideas, and suggestions for relating articles to lectures, cases, and simulations.

ACKNOWLEDGMENTS

Grateful acknowledgment is made to the following people who reviewed various drafts of the manuscript and made helpful recommendations for its improvement:

Jay Azriel
Illinois State University

Rob Blakey
Accenture
San Francisco, CA

Wade M. Danis
Marquette University

Jon Down
Oregon State University

Zane Doyle
Randy Wagner
University of Arizona

Howard D. Feldman
University of Portland

Tom Gilmore
Center for Applied Research
Philadelphia, PA

Bill Hein, Sr.
Pepperdine University (emeritus)

Bob Keidel
Drexel University

Henry Mintzberg
McGill University

Don Smith, Jr.
Carnegie Mellon University/University of Pittsburgh

To my colleagues at the University of the Pacific—Michael Ballot, Arturo Giraldez, Gary Litton, Herb Marshall, Newman Peery, John Pfaff, and Suzanne Walchli—I extend my thanks.

I would also like to thank the many people at South-Western who helped make the book a reality, including Rob Bloom, Molly Flynn, Emma Guttler, Anna Hasselo, Heather Mann, Joe Sabatino, and Erin Williams.

Cynthia Wagner Weick
University of the Pacific

ABOUT THE EDITOR

Cynthia Wagner Weick is Professor of Management at University of the Pacific, in Stockton, California, where she teaches courses in Strategic Management and Policy, Management of Technology and Innovation, and Global Competition. Prior to joining Pacific's faculty in 1990, she served as a corporate planner at Pioneer Hi-Bred International, as a consultant to the United Nations Development Program, and as a Research Scientist at Battelle Columbus Laboratories. Her articles on the use of metaphor in business strategy, and the commercial development of science and technology, have appeared in journals such as *Business Horizons, Technology in Society,* and the *Journal of Creativity and Innovation Management.* Wagner Weick earned her doctorate at the Wharton School, University of Pennsylvania, and her M.S. and B.S. at The Ohio State University.

ABOUT THE CONTRIBUTORS

Min Chen

Min Chen is an associate professor at Thunderbird, the American Graduate School of International Management, where he teaches Negotiation, Foreign Direct Investment Management, Comparative Management, and Asian Business Strategies and Management. His teaching and research have benefited from his unique working experience as Corporate Business Development Vice President of a major American MNC in Asia for more than six years. He has authored and co-authored eight books and more than 40 articles in various journals in both English and Chinese. His books include *Asian Management Systems* and *Managing International Technology Transfer.*

Stephen Cummings

Stephen Cummings is Professor of Strategic Management at Victoria Management School in New Zealand, and a visiting lecturer at MIB, Ecole National Center de Paris and Vlerick Business School, University of Ghent, Belgium. Previous posts include lecturer in corporate strategy at Warwick Business School (WBS) in the United Kingdom and tutor in classical history at Victoria. He is the author of *ReCreating Strategy* and editor of *Images and Strategy.* Cummings has published papers on strategy and its links to ethics, systems thinking, and managing change in journals such as *Harvard Business Review, Long Range Planning, Organization Studies,* and *Business Horizons.*

Kathleen Eisenhardt

Kathleen Eisenhardt is Professor of Strategy and Organization in the Management Science and Engineering Department at Stanford University. She is widely known for her work on strategy, strategic decision making, and innovation in rapidly changing and highly competitive markets. In addition to her many journal publications, she is the coauthor (with Shona L. Brown) of the book *Competing on the Edge: Strategy as Structured Chao*s. She is the recipient of a number of awards, including the Pacific Telesis Foundation Award, the Whittemore Prize (with D. Charles Galunic), and the Stern Award (with Claudia B. Schoonhoven). She is also a Fellow of the Academy of Management.

BRUCE HENDERSON

Bruce Henderson (1915–1992) founded the Boston Consulting Group in 1963, and has been called "the father of strategic consulting." He is credited with inventing and popularizing widely used management concepts such as the experience curve and the BCG growth-share matrix portfolio planning model. Prior to starting BCG, he headed Arthur D. Little's management services unit, and served as a vice president of the Westinghouse Corporation. "The Origin of Strategy" was published when he was nearly 75.

ROBERT KEIDEL

Robert Keidel is Visiting Associate Professor of Management at the LeBow College of Business, Drexel University; and principal of Robert Keidel Associates, in Wyncote, Pennsylvania. He was a Senior Fellow at the Wharton School, University of Pennsylvania; Faculty Fellow at the U.S. Office of Personnel Management; and Program Consultant at the National Center for Productivity & Quality of Working Life. He is a former corporate project manager and naval line officer. In addition to his management books, he has published numerous articles in journals such as *Management Science, Human Relations, Management Review, Organizational Dynamics,* and *Academy of Management Executive.*

HENRY MINTZBERG

Henry Mintzberg is Cleghorn Professor of Management Studies at McGill University in Montreal, where he has taught since 1968. Mintzberg is a noted and prolific author on managerial work, strategy formation, and forms of organizing. He has written more than 120 articles and ten books, including *The Rise and Fall of Strategic Planning*, which won the Academy of Management's Terry Award for best publication by a member in 1995. He has received numerous honorary degrees and awards, including Distinguished Scholar for the year 2000 from the Academy of Management, Officer of the Order of Canada, and l'Ordre National du Quebec. He was also included in a list of the top 50 business intellectuals in 2002 by Accenture's Institute for Strategic Change.

RICHARD RAPAPORT

Richard Rapaport is a freelance writer based in San Francisco. He is also a contributing editor to Forbes ASAP. His political commentary appears frequently in Knight Ridder and other newspaper chains throughout the United States.

ROSALIE TUNG

Rosalie Tung is Professor of International Business at Simon Fraser University (Canada), where she holds the Ming and Stella Wong Chaired Professorship. Dr. Tung is serving as President of the Academy of Management in 2003–2004. She has been elected as a Fellow of the Royal Society of Canada and as a Fellow of the Academy of Management. She has been named as one of the world's five most cited authors in international business by the *Journal of International Business Studies*. Professor Tung has published widely on the subjects of international management and organizational theory in journals such as *Organizational Dynamics, Journal of International Business Studies, Academy of Management Executive*, and *California Management Review*.

INTRODUCTION
BUSINESS IS BUSINESS

"Business is Business," the Little Man said,
"A battle where 'everything goes,'
Where the only gospel is 'get ahead,'
And never spare friends or foes.
'Slay or be slain,' is the slogan cold;
You must struggle and slash and tear,
For Business is Business, a fight for gold,
Where all that you do is fair."

"Business is Business," the Big Man said,
"A battle to make of earth
A place to yield us more clothes and bread,
More pleasure and joy and mirth;
There are still some bandits and buccaneers
Who are jungle-bred beasts of trade,
But their number dwindles with passing years
And dead is the code they made!"

"Business is Business," the Big Man said,
"But it's something that's more, far more;
For it makes sweet gardens of deserts dead,
And cities it built now roar
Where once the deer and gray wolf ran
From the pioneer's swift advance;
Business is magic that toils for man,
Business is True Romance.

"And those who make it a ruthless fight
Have only themselves to blame
If they feel no whit of the keen delight
In playing the Bigger Game,
The game that calls on the heart and head,
The best of man's strength and nerve;
'Business is Business,'" the Big Man said,
"And that business is to serve!"

—Berton Braley (1917)

Business is an unusual topic for a poem. In Berton Braley's hand, however, the genre seems quite natural. His linguistic device, the metaphor, is one we are accustomed to finding in poetry and prose. By taking concepts out of context Braley sets up starkly contrasting images of the purpose and *modus operandi* of business. Within four stanzas laden with metaphoric allusion he makes clear to which sort of business we owe our allegiance: the Bigger Game. Who in their right mind would align themselves with "jungle beasts of trade," when the alternative is "magic," "true romance," and "making gardens of deserts"? By the end of the poem we *think* differently, and perhaps even are motivated to *act* differently. Metaphors do this. They help us conceptualize and communicate ideas vividly and creatively. Metaphors are "an everyday example of creative cognition in action," write Glucksberg *et al.* (1997) "…they are used either to extend established categories or, if no relevant categories exist, to create new ones." Ward *et al.* (1997) view metaphors as "at once evidence of creative functioning in those who produce them, and spurs to creative discovery and enlightenment in those who hear or read them." In *Modern Rhetoric*, Brooks and Warren (1970) suggest that metaphors are effective in large part because "they are concrete and particular; they reflect the world of the senses. They can still excite the imagination."

Braley shows us business can belong in the realm of poetic metaphor. But does metaphor belong in the realm of business? *Out of Context: A Creative Approach to Strategic Management* answers this question with an unequivocal yes. It does so through a collection of readings that offers lessons in strategic management in business from the realms of athletics, the military, philosophy, political theory, evolution, and art. The readings draw from modern and ancient thought, from the East and the West. Metaphor does not substitute for more literal and direct thought and word. However, just as metaphor changed and sharpened the lens through which we see business in Braley's poem, metaphor offers a unique manner of thinking about business strategy. Moreover, it is an approach that the complexity and pace of modern business demands. The challenges faced by business leaders require that we draw upon all the facets we can muster, from as many and as diverse a set of sources as possible. "There is a growing realization," write Akin and Palmer (2000), "that effective managers are able to utilize multiple metaphors to comprehend and manage organizational situations. Use of a limited array of metaphors can trap managers by narrowing the options they perceive as open to them in responding to new (and old) situations. Indeed, whole organizations can become locked culturally into a narrow use of metaphors and a correspondingly narrow view of the organizational world."

The value of metaphor is clear to Sun Microsystems CEO Scott McNealy. "The companies that will succeed," he argues, "will be the ones that make their ideas real, that stand for what is true, and that employ great metaphors and analogies to define their business and tell their stories" (quoted in Forbes ASAP, 2000). McNealy's archrival, Bill Gates, also is no stranger to metaphor. In his 1997 Letter to Shareholders, Gates conveyed his vision for the direction of his company and customers in terms of a "digital nervous system."

We believe that employees are more than cogs in a machine. We believe businesses succeed because of the intelligence and creativity of their employees. We believe that in order for a business to stay competitive in this fast paced world, it needs a digital approach. But to allow our customers to reap the true rewards of building a digital nervous system, we need to get them off the treadmill of having so many of their resources just to keep systems up and running. (Bill Gates, Letter to Shareholders, 1997)

Berkshire Hathaway's Warren Buffet addresses his company's shareholders in what could easily be called business prose. His pithy insights into his company's performance and his picture of the future are peppered with metaphor. For example, in the 2002 Annual Report he explained his view of successful management in terms of baseball.

My managerial model is Eddie Bennett, who was a batboy (someone who picks up the bat after a batter makes a hit and runs off to first base in the sport baseball). In 1919, at age 19, Eddie began his work with the Chicago White Sox, who that year went to the World Series. The next year, Eddie switched to the Brooklyn Dodgers, and they, too, won their league title. Our hero, however, smelled trouble. Changing boroughs, he joined the Yankees in 1921, and they promptly won their first pennant in history. Now Eddie settled in, shrewdly seeing what was coming. In the next seven years, the Yankees won five American League titles. What does this have to do with management? It's simple—to be a winner, work with winners. (Warren Buffet, Letter to the Shareholders, 2002)

Kemira, a $2.5 billion diversified chemical company based in Helsinki, Finland, has taken the use of metaphor to a creative extreme. Facing a future made uncertain by the evolving European Union, Kemira's top managers organized a retreat in which they each literally painted pictures of the company's future. This exercise provided the executives with a vivid medium for expressing their hopes and concerns to their colleagues. The artwork also was used to illustrate Kemira's 2001 Annual Report.

What good is a concept of strategy if it is not effectively communicated and acted upon? In addition to helping a strategist create a novel vision of the future, metaphors may also incite action. In their seminal treatise on linguistics, *Metaphors We Live By*, Lakoff and Johnson (1980) argue that "Much of cultural change arises from the introduction of new metaphorical concepts and the loss of old ones." Akin and Palmer (2000) note that "Metaphors have the effect of both describing and constructing our organizational realities. By naming a situation through a metaphor, we not only give it a rich identity but also engender actions that actually create the reality." Metaphor widens a leader's conceptual and linguistic vocabulary to include vivid means to communicate the often-abstract notions of strategy. Thus, implementation, the Achilles heal of strategy processes, is aided by metaphor.

The metaphor, then, is not only a literary device of the poet writing *about* business, but a tool for the leader creating, communicating, and implementing strategy *within* business. Strategy requires that we learn to look through many lenses, and have many ways of communicating. Therefore, the metaphors that follow in this book come from a wide range of contexts and variety of authors. The more metaphors we have, the more lenses we have to see through, the more mental fodder we have for grasping today's circumstances and for imagining new futures. The larger our vocabulary, the more we can make ourselves understood to a wider variety of people, and find the words that are most likely to incite action.

Out of Context has been organized as a journey in metaphor. The first section, "Well-Trodden Paths," presents metaphors from contexts to which strategists are probably most accustomed—athletics and the military. Section Two, "Alternate Routes," provides approaches to strategy again from the military and from classic Asian sources as well. "Ancient Footprints," the third section, delves into metaphors from 16th-century political theory and Greek philosophy. The fourth section, "Roads Less Traveled," covers approaches to strategy from the contexts of evolutionary biology, pottery-making, and music. The final section, "Endless Journey," provides still another metaphor—strategic impressionism—and challenges strategists to find new metaphors that deepen our understanding of the concepts of strategy, spark creative thinking, and enhance our ability to communicate strategy effectively.

QUESTIONS

1. As you learn about CEOs in *Businessweek, Forbes, Fortune,* or from other sources, what metaphors do you find they use in describing their company strategy? What metaphors do others use to describe these leaders or their approach? Have these metaphors helped create strategic direction for the company? Could these metaphors *limit* the thinking of the leader?

2. Do these CEOs, or others who write about them, discuss what has influenced their thinking? Do they have experience or interest in the military? Athletics? Philosophy? Art, and so on?

3. What metaphors do the leaders in your own organization use? What has influenced their thinking?

1

WELL-TRODDEN PATHS

We have to play this fast paced game of business as Gretzky played hockey. In less than a blink of an eye, we must compute where the puck is likely to end up, based on very subtle indicators related to its current position, and be ready to capture it when it gets there.

—Goett (2000)

Section One includes articles from athletics and the military, contexts from which strategists in business often draw. The first selection applies metaphors from American sports to business. It is followed by an interview with former head football coach, Bill Walsh, who offers his ideas on how to build flexibility and adaptability into traditionally hierarchical sports and companies. The path then turns to military strategy from ancient Greece, where the insights of the Athenian general Pericles clarify how modern Western strategy echoes its Greek roots, but also deviates from them.

In the initial article Robert Keidel contrasts baseball, football, and basketball in terms of the way they are coordinated, and the responsibilities and limitations of their leaders. He shows that lumping together all sports—and the business organizations they mirror—masks important distinctions among them. Like all metaphors, each sport model emphasizes some dimensions, and de-emphasizes or completely neglects others. The role of the strategist in particular varies markedly among the three models. A leader with a "football mentality" is accustomed to devising detailed long-term plans *a priori*, which are then communicated to those lower in the organization's hierarchy who are expected to implement them. How effective would this sort of leader be in a baseball-type company, in which employees expect to operate with a high degree of autonomy? Not very. The strategic role of the leader in the baseball organization lies mostly in choosing individual employees in the first place, after which they have to be satisfied with tactical influence. Neither the football nor the baseball leader would be comfortable in a basketball-type company. Here successful strategists put their energy into ensuring dynamic interrelationships among employees, and constantly "influencing the flow of the game" as it is played.

In addition to matching the mind-sets of leaders to different types of companies, Keidel's article offers insight into the ways a leader must change as a company grows from a small, entrepreneurial firm to one that necessitates increased hierarchy and division of labor. There are many, many examples of failure on the part of a company's founder to lead this growth. Keidel's sports models help explain why this is so, and point to changes in thinking and behavior necessary to achieve success.

Building flexibility into the rigidly structured sport of football is on the mind of coaching legend Bill Walsh in his interview with Richard Rapaport, the second article in this section. Walsh argues that a winning team requires that leaders in sports and business recognize and overcome the limitations of the football model, particularly hierarchy and top-down communication and control. Even leaders of large organizations must be attentive to the need for people to be treated and developed as individuals. To be a successful coach or CEO, leaders must motivate and constantly challenge employees. They must overcome what Walsh terms "the ego barrier," the distraction of one's own importance. Says Walsh, "You are striving for an organization where people understand the importance of their jobs and to taking direction; and an organization where people feel adaptive and are willing to change their minds without feeling threatened. It is a tough combination to achieve … but it's the ultimate in management …. It is the job of the coach to find the best of both sides. We had to have a very structured system of football, and we also wanted instinctive and spontaneous play."

In the third article, Stephen Cummings reaches back to the roots of Western strategy, to the Athenian general and strategist Pericles. "Strategos," Greek for "leading an army" was the basis of both military and political leadership in ancient times. Several dimensions of the Greek concept of strategy reinforce modern notions of strategy in Western companies. The Greeks saw that strategy should not be viewed as a purely rational process that resulted in an overly rigid plan, but that building in flexibility and opportunism was key to success. Pericles believed that strategists must create, articulate, and communicate vision, inspiring others to great heights. However, Cummings points out that we have also deviated from Greek wisdom in a very important way. In ancient Athens the strategist operated in the thick of battle to gain intimate knowledge of circumstances and the actions that needed to be taken, and also to serve as a model to those lower in rank. "Strategy was perceived as a line function, which stands in marked contrast to the contemporary notion of strategic planning as a staff function."

Traveling these well-trodden paths prompts a question. Has strategy based on athletic and military metaphors lost its relevance in modern business? Keidel shows how critical it is to examine the assumptions behind the sports metaphors we use in business. Walsh suggests that hierarchy is being toppled even within football. Are there assumptions behind athletic and military models in general that are inappropriate to the business realm? In business, after all, more than one competitor can win. And the assumption of relentless competition between atomistic companies seems blind to the emphasis on cooperative behavior that has come to characterize business strategy. Moreover, just as a metaphor can inspire, it can also exclude. Will metaphors from athletics and the military be effective in communicating strategy to the wide variety of people in the modern workforce? How consistent is it for a CEO to tout the company's global mind-set, and then describe their strategy in terms of baseball, football, or basketball?

Are athletic and military models still useful to business strategists? Despite the above caveats, yes. The reasons why will become evident as the journey continues.

BASEBALL, FOOTBALL, AND BASKETBALL: MODELS FOR BUSINESS

ROBERT W. KEIDEL

Teamwork and hustle ... game plans and goal line stands ... playing hardball in the big leagues. Not only is professional sports a business; it is an exemplar for business. Indeed, if it can be said that nature follows art, then surely business must follow sports. How many executives, for instance, strive for the historical precision of the Dallas Cowboys or the cohesiveness of the Boston Celtics? How many deep down see themselves as corporate Billy Cunninghams, George Allens, or Whitey Herzogs? Probably quite a few.

Business's identification with sports, sports teams, and sports personalities is pervasive. None of this is lost on periodicals like *Sports Illustrated*, which touts its "speakers bureau" of 2,000 sports stars "ready to sparkle at sales meetings, award dinners, conventions, store openings, or wherever else the color and excitement of sports, can help you shine."

For most managers, sports' relevance to running a business consists of global concepts like "team spirit," "competitiveness," and "winning." Something more, however, is suggested by the use of sport-specific metaphors like "home run hitter," "quarterback," or "point guard." I believe that managers' habitual use of such metaphors suggests an identification with a particular sport, which may then be projected onto their organizations. Thus, a manager constantly in search of a "stopper" may be projecting an uncritical baseball-team view of behavior onto his or her organizational world.

Such projection may be of little consequence, especially if the sports image is highly generalized. However, if the sports image is rather specific and if it corresponds more to a decision maker's personality than to organizational reality, it could cause trouble. Consider the following cases:

■ The operations vice-president of a durable-goods producer was convinced that the best guarantee of effective manufacturing was an overachieving plant manager. When one of his plants—a highly integrated, high volume facility—ran into difficulties, he quickly inserted a new, more ambitious plant manager. Six months later, with the plant still floundering, the director declared: "I've had it with singles hitters; I need someone who can turn it around with one swing." Thereupon he brought in still another manager, even more aggressive than his predecessor. The decline continued. As the plant's production control staff later recounted, the problem was never the plant manager; it was an incomprehensible production/inventory control system that no one—at the plant or at corporate headquarters—had ever really understood. Unfortunately, the vice-president's "long-ball" model, in

Reprinted from *Organizational Dynamics*, Winter, Robert W. Keidel, "Baseball, Football and Basketball: Models for Business," pp 5–18 (1984), with permission from Elsevier Science.

which the crucial individual would carry the day, prevented him from seeing this.

- The president of a high-technology marketing firm sought to imbue a "total team concept" throughout his organization. His model was basketball: close teamwork and cooperation among all organizational units. The company's structure, however, worked against this. Units were geographically scattered across the country, and each operated quasi-autonomously. They rarely interacted with each other and in fact perceived themselves (correctly) to be in competition with each other for corporate recognition and resources. Hence, attempts to inspire a sense of "all-for-one" were set up to fail, and did.

- The corporate training director of a leading office systems company believed that the twin keys to managerial success were "clear direction and precise execution." This individual had attended a university renowned for its football prowess. While not a football player himself, he had identified with the sport and with his university's team. This identification carried with him into business. He organized a series of corporation-wide training seminars featuring videotapes of prominent football coaches. The basic pitch was "You need a quarterback and you need to pull together as a team." These seminars may have had a positive effect on some, but they became a standing joke among the company's large population of self-starting individual contributors, who ranged from entry-level salesmen to solid-state physicists.

- The leader of a multi-disciplinary management-consulting team on location at a client's site abruptly resigned. He was replaced by the most senior member of the project team. The new leader brought together all project staff to explain his approach to management: "When you have a team of Mike Schmidts, Dave Parkers, Johnny Benches ... you don't manage them. You just let them play. Well, that's what you guys are. You're all-stars. You can manage by yourselves." Several consultants took this literally. They began to work more and more on their own, just as the project demanded greater collaboration across disciplines. The client organization soon became dissatisfied with the overall consulting performance and terminated the engagement.

As compelling as the above cases are, the significant point is not that managers have done damage by applying inappropriate sports notions. What is significant is the opportunity that managers have to actually learn from sports. The three major professional team sports in the United States—baseball, football, and basketball—exhibit profoundly different dynamics and exemplify three organizational patterns common in business (and other sectors). Each represents a model—a coherent set of relationships that captures the essence of an organizational form. By studying these models, managers can gain new insight into their own organizations—and possibly their own cognitive orientations.

Each model is grounded in a particular kind of internal "interdependence." This idea has to do with how parts (or members) of an organization interact. In pooled interdependence, there is little or no interaction; the parts act more or less independently of each other. In sequential interdependence, the parts interact in series: A feeds B, which in turn feeds C, and so on. In reciprocal interdependence, each part interacts with every other. The flow is back-and-forth.

In fact, each sport contains examples of every form of interdependence. For instance, each displays reciprocal interdependence because offense and defense always feed each other. Granted this, however, significant differences separate professional baseball, football, and basketball. These differences are summarized in Exhibit 1, which sketches the three organizational models. In the rest of this article I will explore these models by (1) contrasting team structures and the latters' implications for team management and (2) detailing the relevance of the sports models to business management.

TEAM STRUCTURE

Each of the three professional sports has a unique structure. Here are the relevant details.

BASEBALL Of the three sports, professional baseball exhibits the greatest degree of pooled interdependence. Team-member contributions are relatively independent of each other. In the words of Pete Rose, "Baseball is a team game, but nine men who reach their individual goals make a nice team." Where interaction does occur, it is usually between no more than two or three players (on the same team)—for example, pitcher-catcher, batter-base runner, infielder-infielder. Rarely are more than a few of the players on the field involved directly in a given play—outside of making adjustments in fielding positions in anticipation of a play (or to back up a play).

EXHIBIT 1	THREE ORGANIZATIONAL MODELS		
	Sports		
Dimension	**Baseball**	**Football**	**Basketball**
Dominant interdependence	Pooled	Sequential	Reciprocal
Density	Low	Moderate	High
Basic unit	Individual	Group	Team
Key coordination mechanism	Design of sport	Planning and hierarchy	Mutual adjustment
Core management competence	Tactical	Strategic	Integrative
Developmental focus	Individual	Individual and group	Individual and team

The geographical dispersion of the players in baseball is also the least dense of the three sports. Players are spread across a wide playing area, especially in the "outfield." This widespread placement, combined with low interaction, makes a baseball team—and a baseball game—a "loosely coupled" system. Spatial separation is mirrored by the relation between offense and defense: They are totally separate or "disjointed." The contest is stopped while one team leaves the field and the other takes it.

The basic unit in baseball is the individual. More so than in either football or basketball, overall performance approximates the sum of team members' performances. This is vividly demonstrated by the way offense works: Players come up to bat one at a time. Of course, scoring typically requires a sequence of actions such as walks, hits, and sacrifices. But individual contributions remain rather discrete.

FOOTBALL Professional football exhibits sequential interdependence in two ways. First, on offense, the line leads ("feeds") the backfield by providing the blocking necessary for running and passing. Second, in a more fundamental sense, the flow of plays usually required to score—that is, a linear series of "first downs" across a "gridiron"—could not be more sequential.

The dispersion of the players in football is denser than in baseball. Football involves twice as many players on a smaller field. Most players—the lines, offensive backs and, to an extent, the linebackers—are usually bunched together. Further, all players on the field are involved in every play. In two words, football is "tightly coupled."

Moreover, there is a continuous element of contingency as to who controls the ball. Offense and defense can turn into each other at any time as a result of a turnover (a fumble or an interception). Apart from turnovers, the (normal) transition game has become a third component of football, linking offense and defense. Transitions are frequently played by specialists, members of "special teams" who may have made the squad solely on the basis of their play in this facet of the game.

The basic units in football are the large group or platoon (offense, defense, and transition) and, to a lesser degree, the small group (linemen, linebackers, backfield, and so forth). Overall performance is basically the sum of the platoons' performances. Each platoon's challenge is to be as machinelike as possible—a metaphor that is especially apt for this sport. It is instructive to picture the football field as a factory, with the moving line of scrimmage representing product flow through the factory. According to George Allen, then-head coach of the Washington Redskins:

> A football team is a lot like a machine. It's made up of parts. If one part doesn't work, one player pulling against you and not doing his job, the whole machine fails.

BASKETBALL Professional basketball exhibits a high degree of reciprocal interdependence, as demonstrated by the back-and-forth flow of the ball among players. The reciprocal character of the sport is also shown in the often frenetic movement up and down the court—a far cry from the deliberate, measured advance of a classic football scoring drive.

The dispersion of players in basketball is the most dense of the three sports. Like football, basketball is also tightly coupled. But the coupling differs. In football, players are coupled to their individual roles, as though programmed; in basketball, players are coupled to all of their teammates in a fluid, unfolding manner. Every player (1) is involved in offense, defense, and transition; (2) handles the ball; and (3) attempts to score.

If offense and defense are "linked" in football, they are overlapping or "intersecting" in basketball. Offense and defense may turn into each other instantaneously, and often do. The transition game is not a separate piece with separate players, as it is in football; it is continuous, part of the flow. Indeed, a fast-breaking professional basketball game gives the sensation of an electronic video game.

The basic unit in basketball is the team. With only five players on the court, an intermediate grouping between the team and the individual is unrealistic. Unit performance therefore is a function of player interaction, where each player may be involved with every other player on the court.

The means/end structures of the three sports are depicted graphically in Exhibit 2. In baseball, team outcome—a win or a loss—is the aggregate of individual (and small group) efforts. It is predominantly the sum of individual v. individual (pitcher v. batter) confrontations. In football, team outcome is the aggregate of platoon performances. The dominant competition is group v. group (offense v. defense, special team v. special team). Finally, in basketball, team outcome is not an aggregate of subunits' performances; it is a function of team performance—player actions and especially, interactions. The dominant competition is team v. team (encompassing offense, defense, and transition).

IMPLICATIONS FOR TEAM MANAGEMENT

These structural differences make a difference in the way teams are managed in the three sports. Implications concern coordination, management competence, and developmental focus.

EXHIBIT 2	THREE MEANS/END STRUCTURES

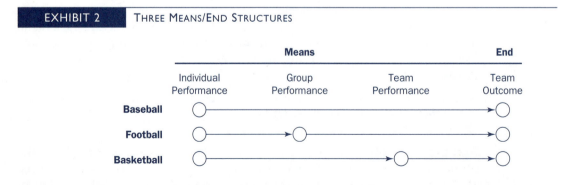

BASEBALL In baseball, coordination is achieved primarily through the design (structure) of the game. There are no "game plans" or overarching strategies to devise—with the possible exception of pitching rotation. Game related decisions are tactical, both before the start of the contest (filling out a lineup card) and during it (making substitutions, positioning fielders, pitching out, pinch hitting, advancing a runner, and so forth). The core management competence is the ability to make episodic judgments in real time. The effective manager in baseball may be described as a "tactician."

Because a baseball team is loosely coupled, instilling team—or, at least, team manager—cohesiveness may not be critical. Indeed, one can find evidence for the opposite conclusion—that is to say, a disruptive manager may succeed in part by stirring things up. Billy Martin and Dallas Green, who won World Series with the Yankees and the Phillies, respectively, are two cases in point. The value (or irrelevance) of disruptiveness may extend even to owners, as witness Charley Finley and George Steinbrenner. Concerning Steinbrenner, an editorial in *The Wall Street Journal* speculates: "Do the Yankees succeed despite their boss's nastiness, or because of it? The idea that nice guys finish last ... isn't new by any means, but it has been brought home with particular force in sports of late."

Because baseball's basic unit is the individual player, developmental efforts focus primarily on honing individual skills. Clearly, certain interactions (double plays, pickoff attempts, relay throws, and so forth) are important. But these tend to involve few players and significantly, depend more on individual execution than on interaction.

FOOTBALL Coordination in football is achieved through planning and hierarchical direction. Of the three sports, only professional football is strategy-intensive at the game level. This is a function of both the "strategic" importance of each contest and the nature of the sport. The National Football League's regular season consists of 16 games, as compared with 82 in the National Basketball Association and 162 in major league baseball; hence, the average football game has five times the significance of a basketball game and ten times that of a baseball game. Moreover, in the post-season playoffs, a football team is eliminated by a single loss, whereas at each step in the elimination process baseball and basketball teams play the best of a series.

In football, films of the upcoming opponent are run and rerun to provide clues as to likely play sequences, formations, coverages, and so on. The team's own previous performance is also reviewed, a game plan is formulated, and players are drilled exhaustively in anticipation. In neither of the other two sports are instructions for each play so precise, or job descriptions so narrow. Football's combination of meticulous preparation, high information volume, and fractionated tasks helps to explain why there is much more of a coaching hierarchy in this sport than in baseball or basketball.

The primary unit to be internally coordinated is the group. Indeed, player identification with the group, especially the platoon—whether offense, defense, or transition—may be more readily achieved than identification with the team as a whole. It may also be at least as valuable: Interplatoon rivalry within a team can physically and psychologically prepare players for the conflict of the next game. Thus, reports that fights are breaking out as offense and defense "bang on each other" during practice may be a positive sign. In any case, the platoon's integrity is central; developing cohesiveness within it is an essential management task.

BASKETBALL The key coordinating mechanism in basketball is mutual adjustment by the players. The coach's tasks are (1) to develop the team's ability to adjust and (2) to intervene (during a game) on an exception basis. Indeed, the game strategy of the effective basketball coach often resembles that of the counterpuncher in boxing: It is a "planned reaction." And while his or her counterpart in baseball must make a flow of adjustments to specific game situations, the basketball coach must make adjustments to the flow of the overall game (through time outs, match-up changes, and so forth).

In basketball, interaction is more important than the sum of individual players' actions. Thus it is often said that the core skill in basketball is passing, which requires continuous movement by all—not just by the player with the ball. An effective passing game diminishes the need for outstanding shooters or (offensive) rebounders because it produces dunks and layups—high-percentage shots.

To achieve the dynamic interaction required in professional basketball demands interpersonal as well as technical competence on the part of the coach. The coach must be acutely sensitive to personality nuances and be able to blend very different types—especially because the placement of players in basketball is so dense. Indeed, more than any other sport, basketball appears to parallel Japanese industry (and society): Cooperation at close quarters is a matter of survival. In sum, the successful basketball coach knows how to cohere. The coach is— psychosocially as well as technically—an "integrator."

As indicated, the basic unit in basketball is the team. Individual development must take place within this context. In terms of individual/team primacy, basketball is the opposite of baseball. A teamful of prima donnas can win it all in baseball; this is less likely in basketball. As Bill Bradley pointed out in 1977—after the talent-laden Philadelphia 76ers had lost in the NBA finals to the Portland Trailblazers—"Maybe someday a team will have so much individual firepower that on that alone it can win a championship. It hasn't happened yet." It still hasn't.

SPORTS AS MODELS FOR BUSINESS

Professional team sports are a fertile laboratory for managers because they mirror business. Despite obvious differences—for example, few businesses operate within such narrow parameters as those governing sports teams—the parallels are striking. At a general level they concern (1) the need to compete externally, (2) the need to cooperate internally, (3) the need to manage human resources strategically, and (4) generic structure.

First, sports exemplify competition. All businesses face intensifying international competition for markets and resources. Sports provide a crucible in which to witness competition in a concentrated form. Business (and other) organizations can observe competitive lessons in sharp relief by critically viewing sports contests—especially because results are unambiguous.

Second, sports exemplify cooperation. One of team sports' major lessons is that regardless of task requirements, some measure of cooperation is crucial to competitiveness. Sports provide the opportunity to comprehend teamwork in an array of concrete forms (within each sport as well as between sports.) This actual variety contrasts sharply with the vague and undifferentiated sense in which "teamwork" tends to be used.

Third, sports are human resources strategic. In each of the three sports, the management of human resources is a central part of overarching strategy—especially because: (1) strategic decisions take place within a (sport, league, season, and game) framework already mandated, and (2) sports are unequivocally "people-intensive." The net effect is that sports provides a direct window on strategic human resources management.

Finally, sports encompass generic group structures. The size range of baseball, football, and basketball teams—from five to eleven players in action (and from 12 to 47 players in total)—parallels the size range of most organizational building-block groups (work clusters, departments, project teams, and so forth) in business.

At a specific level, baseball, football, and basketball represent models that can help managers understand how their organizations work. For all complex businesses are made up of disparate units, some of which resemble baseball teams, others football teams, and still others basketball teams. Articulating the resemblances can clarify managements' charge.

What are the relevant criteria? Essentially they are the dimensions listed in Exhibit 1, which may be recast as a checklist for selecting a model—or for assessing the appropriateness of a model in use. Exhibit 3 summarizes unit properties of "baseball," "football," and "basketball" companies.

While this display is worded in terms of intra-unit relations, it applies as well to inter-unit relations, where player:team is equivalent to unit:organization. Some examples will illustrate.

BASEBALL-COMPANIES Organizations that fit this type are loosely coupled. They include the classic sales organization, made up of high-performing soloists. Also within this category are aggregations of basic researchers, in which each individual independently pursues his or her own line of inquiry—as happens with university professors. At a more macro level, organizations with dispersed, quasi-autonomous units—geographically organized firms, holding companies, franchise-based operations—likewise have much in common with a baseball team. The whole is roughly the sum of its parts (units).

EXHIBIT 3	A DIAGNOSTIC CHECKLIST		
	Baseball-Company	**Football-Company**	**Basketball-Company**
1. What is the nature (and degree) of task-based interaction among unit members?	Pooled (low).	Sequential (moderate).	Reciprocal (high).
2. What is the geographical distribution of unit members?	Widely dispersed.	Somewhat clustered.	Highly concentrated.
3. Given company objectives and constraints, where does the autonomy reside?	Within each member unit.	Above the unit (that is, within unit management).	Among the unit members (that is, within the unit as a whole).
4. How is coordination achieved?	Through the unit design in which the sum of individual unit members' objectives approximates unit objectives.	Through complex protocols that clearly and tightly specify the roles and responsibilities of each unit member.	Through continuous self-regulation and responsibility sharing among unit members.
5. What words best describe unit structure?	Network/ conglomerate.	Bureaucratic/ mechanistic.	Adhocratic/organic.
6. What sports expression metaphorically sums up the operating management task?	Fill out (revise) the line-up card.	Prepare (execute) the game plan.	Influence the game's flow.

FOOTBALL-COMPANIES Companies within this cluster tend to have "long-linked" technologies; that is, their production processes involve a complex of discrete steps, tightly coupled in serial (and sometimes parallel) order. The most obvious example is the mass assembly line. In general, organizations that can be described as "machine bureaucracies," to use Henry Mintzberg's term, resemble football teams. At a macro level, two varieties of football-like organization can be identified: (1) the vertically integrated firm and (2) the large construction (power plants, ships, high-rise buildings, and so forth) firm. In each case effective performance depends on the ability to orchestrate a complicated but predictable set of activities in careful sequence.

BASKETBALL-COMPANIES Organizations of this sort are tightly coupled but less than tightly hierarchical. They depend more on member interaction than on managerial direction. Examples range from think-tank consulting firms, to creative advertising agencies, to state-of-the-art computer manufacturers. An analogue within more conventional organizations is the ad hoc task force that cuts across levels and functions, and in which all members interact with each other in virtually all aspects of problem-solving activity. Basketball-companies resemble (sets of) autonomous work teams: They are self-organizing and highly flexible.

DISCUSSION

Although no organizational unit can possibly perfectly fit any one configuration, resemblance to a particular sport can highlight salient features previously obscured. Thus, each business situation cited at the beginning of this article calls for a model quite different from the one in use by the manager. (By referencing each of the four cases mentioned there to Exhibit 3, it is evident that the more appropriate models are, respectively, football, baseball, baseball, and basketball.)

One caution must be raised here. When making comparisons with a sports team, it is important to be clear about both the nature of the similarity and the organizational level of analysis. For instance, Ray Kroc, the founder of McDonald's and owner of the San Diego Padres baseball team, opined that "A well-run restaurant is like a winning baseball team; it makes the most of every crew member's talent and takes advantage of every split-second opportunity to speed up service." I believe that McDonald's as a whole does resemble a baseball team in two respects: (1) Corporate management effectively "fills out the line-up card" by authorizing franchises, and (2) each store operates relatively autonomously—with minimal interaction among stores—within a preset design (that is, a corporate-imposed set of rules to insure consistency). Within each store, however, the (corporate-determined) structure and process more closely resemble football (which unlike baseball, does have a game clock). Technologies are highly programmed, individual responsibilities are narrowly specified, and the overall operation amounts to what Theodore Levitt has called a "production-line approach to service." It is fitting that the title of Kroc's autobiography is a football expression, *Grinding It Out: The Making of McDonald's* (Contemporary Books, 1977).

PRACTICAL IMPLICATIONS OF THE SPORTS MODELS

The baseball, football, and basketball models have practical managerial implications.

INDIVIDUAL-ORGANIZATION FIT An organization that resembles a baseball team can and probably should concentrate on technical and individual criteria in assessing a prospective employee. On the whole, a person's desire and ability to function autonomously are more important in this sport than in the other two. Author John Updike has observed that:

> ... of all team sports, baseball, with its graceful intermittences of action, its immense and tranquil field sparsely settled with poised men in white, its dispassionate mathematics, seems to be best suited to accommodate, and be ornamented by, a loner. It is an essentially lonely game.

An organization rather like a football or basketball team must also pay special attention to nontechnical and interpersonal criteria. How compatible will this person be with the firm's "system" (important in both sports) and with its management style (critical in basketball)?

According to Irv Cross, a former all-pro defensive back who began his National Football League career with the Philadelphia Eagles, "an Eagles player could never make an easy transition to the Dallas Cowboys; the systems and philosophies are just too different." By contrast, any major league baseball player can move to any other team in his league and face only minor adjustments. He will find differences in the new home park (weather, turf, lighting, outfield distances, and so forth), but not much else.

DEVELOPMENTAL FLEXIBILITY Because of its loose coupling, a baseball-like organization has considerable flexibility in deciding whether to develop primarily through new hires or through existing personnel. For the same reason, such an organization is also vulnerable to losing key individuals. Some teams—most notably the Los Angeles Dodgers—succeed by developing young players within their own organization and reinforcing a sense of "family." But building a spirit of togetherness is no easy matter given the sport's individualistic structure. Baseball does seem to lend itself to free agency. Effective managers often take advantage. Thus, in the words of the former Baltimore Orioles manager, Earl Weaver, whose career-winning percentage (.596) is the third highest in major league history:

> A manager's job is to select the best players for what he wants done. A manager wins games in December. He tries not to lose them in July. You win pennants in the off-season when you build your team with trades or free agents. They're not all great players, but they can all do something.

By contrast, the relatively tightly coupled character of football and basketball will likely continue to militate against winning through acquisition.

The organizational coherence that football and basketball require favors internal development. Development from within has been a hallmark of most of the consistently successful professional football coaches—for example, Vince Lombardi, Tom Landry, Don Shula, Bud Grant, Chuck Noll. That is, they worked with what they had inherited (or assembled) and from the college draft, rather than from trades. Although the record in professional basketball is mixed, the sport's coaching legend, Red Auerbach of the Boston Celtics, also did it from within—often with draft choices that other teams had passed over. Of course, the small size of a basketball team means that one or two key additions can make a dramatic difference, and there are several examples of successful teams put together through trades. But acquisitions that do work out tend to be interpersonally as well as technically "correct."

MANAGERIAL CONTINUITY In baseball-companies, managerial continuity appears to be unimportant. Manager turnover in the major leagues mirrors player turnover. Going into the 1983 season, only two managers—the Dodgers' Tom Lasorda and the Pirates' Chuck Tanner—had been with their club for as many as seven years. While Lasorda and Tanner—and the Orioles' Weaver—are evidence that continuity can be beneficial, there is abundant alternative evidence that it is not essential.

Professional football stands in apparent contrast to baseball. Teams that have succeeded over the long haul have tended to do so under the same head coach (Lombardi, Landry, Shula, Grant, Noll, and others). It can be argued simply that winning coaches keep their jobs, while losers do not. Without question there is a lot of truth to this. Still, one wonders whether certain chronically marginal teams might not have fared better had they invested in greater coaching stability, especially since each coaching change typically brings with it a new system and the need to build a new culture.

In contrast, the loosely knit character of baseball renders managerial changes less consequential. Thus, several teams have succeeded under several managers; on the other hand, several managers—for example, Billy Martin, Gene Mauch, Dick Williams, have succeeded with several teams. Professional basketball again presents a mixed record. But it is difficult to dismiss the example of Auerbach, under whom the Celtics won nine championships in a ten season stretch.

UNIT PERFORMANCE INCENTIVES In a baseball-company, bonuses reflecting unit performance make little sense because individual contributions are relatively discrete. And where individual performance is closely linked to team outcome (as with a pitcher's win/loss record), the connection is relatively direct; hence, it is adequately recognized by a reward system that is individually based.

In a football-company, there is logic for unit performance incentives, especially where groups within the unit are highly functionally interdependent. Where groups are more independent than interdependent (as is the case with a football team's platoons), bonuses might be group-based in order to capitalize on individual identification with this sub-unit level.

Finally, a basketball-company seems to be made for unit performance incentives insofar as individual contributions defy neat separation. Because such organizations depend on mutual adjustment, there is a rationale for mutualism in reward systems.

COORDINATION The nature and degree of a manager's control will vary with the sport his or her organization parallels. The management task may be conceptualized as a response to organizational requirements for (1) managerial coordination and (2) member coordination involving individuals or units. Baseball, football, and basketball are arrayed against these dimensions in Exhibit 4.

Baseball presents the fewest demands along either dimension. The game's design diminishes the need for managerial coordination; its loosely coupled character also renders member (player) coordination only marginally important. On the surface, the baseball manager's job appears to be easy. In fact, it is exasperating, precisely because he can control so little. A key prerequisite for managing a baseball-like organization, then, is the ability to accept these limits (and function tactically within them).

Football calls for special competence in managerial coordination—so much so that only a moderate degree of member coordination remains necessary. Indeed, despite the size and complexity of his job, the successful football coach may exercise more control over his team than either of his counterparts.

EXHIBIT 4   DIFFERENTIAL COORDINATION REQUIREMENTS

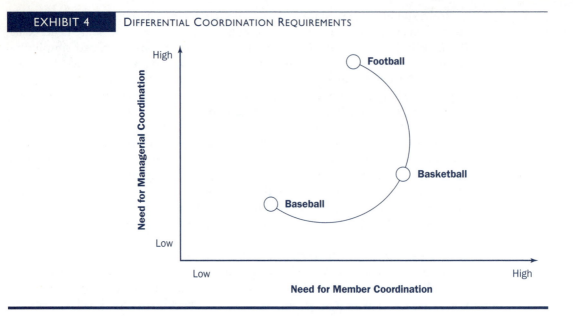

There is a low-to-moderate need for managerial coordination in basketball. What the sport really demands is member coordination—especially during spontaneous (that is, nonprogrammed) activity. The basketball coach can rely far less than the football coach on rehearsals because too much of the game is emerging and unpredictable; unlike football teams, basketball teams do not pause and regroup after each play. The best the basketball coach can do—and what the best coaches always do—is help the players learn how to coordinate themselves.

The sports models' practical implications for business organizations are condensed in Exhibit 5.

CONCLUDING COMMENTS

In this article I have argued that professional baseball, football, and basketball teams represent models that parallel business organizations. Clearly, the likenesses are inexact: No sport can perfectly simulate a business. But I believe that the metaphorical value of sports exceeds this liability. Thomas Peters and Robert Waterman, in their best-seller, *In Search of Excellence* (Harper & Row, 1982), argue that:

> ... people reason intuitively. They reason with simple decision rules, which is a fancy way of saying that, in this complex world, they trust their gut. We need ways of sorting through the infinite minutiae out there, and we start with heuristics—associations, analogues, metaphors ...

At the same time, the business organization, unlike its counterpart in professional sports, is able to change its structure and indeed, its purpose. Thus, a

EXHIBIT 5	PRACTICAL ORGANIZATION OF THE SPORTS MODELS		
	Baseball	**Football**	**Basketball**
Importance of individual-organizational "fit"	Low	Moderate to high	High
Developmental flexibility (from outside v. from within)	High	Low to moderate	Moderate
Importance of managerial continuity	Low	Moderate to high	Moderate
Logic for unit-based performance incentives	Low	Moderate to high	High
Need for managerial coordination	Low	High	Low to moderate
Need for member coordination	Low	Moderate	High

baseball-company seeking to develop deeper employee commitment can take systemic measures to reduce drift or destructive internal competition among roles or units. Alternatively, a football- or basketball-company can take very different steps to increase individual autonomy and accountability. In these and other cases, the business organization has the opportunity to use a sports team as a mirror in diagnosing itself and then proceed to make choices that transcend the model.

It is a well-established fact that psychologically removing a person from a familiar context (business) can stimulate learning about that context. Anxieties and constraints diminish as a fresh perspective opens up. Sports can provide just such a vantage—especially since this realm is so pleasurable for so many. Critical analyses that a manager might resist when applied to his or her own company are welcomed when applied to a sports team. Paradoxically, the relevance of such analyses to the business organization may then become inescapable. In this way, sports can serve as a heuristic medium for business—and other—organizations. Sports truly are user-friendly.

TO BUILD A WINNING TEAM: AN INTERVIEW WITH HEAD COACH BILL WALSH

RICHARD RAPAPORT

Joining the august company of Knute Rockne, Paul Brown, and Vince Lombardi, former San Francisco 49ers and Stanford University football coach Bill Walsh is recognized as one of the most important figures in football history. Walsh, like other coaching legends, has done far more than produce consistently winning teams: in his case, three Super Bowl championships for the 49ers in eight years and an organization enshrined in the press as "The Team of the '80s." During his ten year career with the 49ers and as a coach at the high school, college, and professional levels, Walsh developed a uniquely thoughtful style of play and a successful system of team management that has become one of the most respected in the modern game.

Less of a psychologist than Rockne, and never a disciplinarian like Lombardi, Walsh nevertheless produces winners through a businesslike approach to maximizing the potential of players and coaches. His ability to coolly analyze opponents, matching their weaknesses with his teams' strengths, has made come-from-behind wins a Walsh football hallmark.

Believed to be too cerebral for a top position for which extreme macho was long considered an ineluctable quality, for years Walsh was forced to content himself with assistant coaching positions. Prized nonetheless for his skills on offense, Walsh was honored for honing All-Pro quarterbacks Dan Fouts, Kenny Anderson, and Greg Cook.

In 1977, at age 47, Walsh became Stanford's head football coach. That year, he took a moderately talented Stanford team to a national ranking and a win in the Bluebonnet Bowl. In 1979, Walsh was named head coach and general manager of a dreadful 49ers team that had been virtually dismembered in the late 1970s by mismanagement and horrendous personnel decisions.

Walsh immediately began to develop long-range strategic and personnel plans for the 49ers. He also focused on what other coaches had considered the minutiae of the game: minute-by-minute choreographing of practices, breaking down individual and group tactics into parts, and defining responsibilities and setting objectives for both players and coaches.

Retiring after his third Super Bowl victory in January 1989, Walsh signed on as a football analyst for NBC Sports, eschewing numerous bids to coach professionally before stunning the football world in 1992 by returning as head coach at Stanford.

This interview was conducted by Richard Rapaport.

HBR (*Harvard Business Review*): *Do you see a link between managing and coaching?*

Bill Walsh: I see coaches and executives who have more similar skills today than ever before. When I was with the 49ers, I was both head coach and general manager, so my duties were more business oriented than those of a lot of NFL head coaches. Today's NFL is a very complex world, and great football knowledge alone won't get your team to the Super Bowl.

Historically in sports, there has been one central figure in the organization whose presence dominates everything and whose judgments people identify with. That one person is the dictator, and everyone else simply does whatever he says. In a lot of ways, the old system was much easier for all involved. The dictator gave orders and everyone else just followed them.

Now, working successfully with the people in the organization demands more from the coach or the executive. In coaching, I think of it as the coach's ability to condition the athletes' minds and to train them to think as a unit, while at the same time, making sure each athlete approaches his own game with total concentration, intensity, and skill. There should never be a moment on the football field when a player doesn't feel challenged both physically and intellectually. That is why the old bludgeon approach is leaving football the same way it is leaving business.

What is replacing the old approach?

Management today recognizes that to have a winning organization, it has to be more knowledgeable and competent in dealing with and developing people. That is the most fundamental change. The real task in sports is to bring together groups of people to accomplish something. In the old days, the approach was rather crude. The organization would simply discard a player who did not fit a specific, predefined mold. If a player did not conform to the way management wanted him to behave, or if he made the organization uncomfortable, it got rid of him. That was the typical response.

Today, in sports as elsewhere, individualism is the general rule. Some of the most talented people are the ones who are the most independent. That has required from management a fundamental change in the art and skill of communication and in organizational development. Most important, there has been much more recognition and acknowledgment of the uniqueness of each individual and the need that people have for some degree of security.

How does that translate into winning teams?

Those teams that have been most successful are the ones that have demonstrated the greatest commitment to their people. They are the ones that have created the greatest sense of belonging. And they are the ones that have done the most in-house to develop their people. That commitment has come through in the personality of the organizations. It is true of the Redskins, the Raiders, and, of course, the 49ers.

What is the biggest obstacle to creating this kind of organization?

The coach must account for his ego. He has to drop or sidestep the ego barrier so that people can communicate without fear. They have to be comfortable that they will not be ridiculed if they turn out to be mistaken or if their ideas are not directly in line with their superior's. That is where the breakthrough comes. That is what it takes to build a successful, winning organization.

That approach was certainly critical to the success of the 49ers. It contributed to an environment where our team could be more flexible and adaptable in responding to the unexpected moves of our opponents.

I tried to remove the fear factor from people's minds so they could feel comfortable opening their mouths. They knew they could be wrong one time and then, when they got a little more information, change their opinion and not be demeaned for it. In fact, I made a point of reminding our coaching staff that I expected them to change their opinions and impressions over time. It's quite natural: the more information you develop, the faster things can change.

But having enormous self-confidence seems essential for a leader—especially in pro sports. What is the role of healthy versus unhealthy ego in a competitive organization like a football team?

English is a marvelous language until it comes to the word "ego." We Americans throw that around, using that one word to cover a broad spectrum of meanings: self-confidence, self-assurance, and assertiveness—attributes that most people think of as positive.

But there is another side that can wreck a team or an organization. That is being distracted by your own importance. It can come from your insecurity in working with others. It can be the need to draw attention to yourself in the public arena. It can be a feeling that others are a threat to your own territory. These are all negative manifestations of ego, and if you are not alert to them, you get diverted and your work becomes diffused. Ego in these cases makes people insensitive to how they work with others and ends up interfering with the real goal of any group efforts.

What do you think are the essential management skills of a successful head coach?

The role of the head coach begins with setting a standard of competence. You have to exhibit a strong working knowledge of the game. The head coach must be able to function effectively and decisively in the most stressful situations. And the head coach must demonstrate resourcefulness—in particular, he is responsible for designing a system of football that is not simplistic. The head coach's system should never reduce the game to the point where he can blame his players for success or failure simply because they did not physically overwhelm the opponents.

Successful coaches realize that winning teams are not run by single individuals who dominate the scene and reduce the rest of the group to marionettes. Winning teams are more like open forums in which everyone participates in the

THE TURNAROUND CEO

By 1979, when I came to the 49ers, things were about as bad with the team as they could get. The 49ers fans had been let down so far that they had become indifferent to what was happening with the team. I knew we couldn't take them down even farther by telling them, "Now we're really rebuilding." They had been handed that line from the previous management and coaching staff for the past several years. We couldn't tear the team apart and expect people to come to the games, see a competitive contest, and enjoy themselves.

I didn't have a master plan. It was simply a matter of staying afloat while we prepared for the future. We had to field an entertaining and competitive team, but what we really had in mind was building toward a championship future.

I knew we couldn't get there simply by spending money. Money is an important facet, of course, but you need skill, confidence, and training to win football games. When the 49ers' breakthrough season came in 1981, we won our first championship with the lowest salary schedule in the NFL.

My first two seasons taught me that even in defeat you can make progress if you have confidence, patience, a plan, and a timetable. One of the biggest problems in coaching is the people around you who don't understand what it takes to get the job done or who lose their nerve. There are always quick fixes and instant criticisms that get written up in the sports pages. Head coaches get pressure from ownership, from fans, from the press, from assistant coaches, and from players. They may think you are moving too fast or not fast enough. The owners are often the worst. The team is their investment, so nerves and ego get in the way. They have to feel they have you under their thumbs when they hire you and when they fire you.

With 49ers owner Eddie DeBartolo, Jr., I tried to make sure that he had something in writing in front of him, a plan that we had developed and were implementing. I wrote an operations manual, a personnel manual, a budget manual, and an overall set of job descriptions. I outlined the job of each player, evaluated each member of the team, and set down our goals and expectations for where we were and where we wanted to be. A high degree of documentation gives an owner the feeling that his or her investment is in good hands. Fortunately for me, Eddie never interfered with the changes I wanted to make. He listened and was enthusiastic—at least in the early years. Later he didn't listen quite so well.

In the face of all that, you have got to be resolute in where you are heading and how you plan to get there. And even though you might fail, even though it might not develop, you never panic. A lot of people bring on failure in the way they react to pressure. Most coaches lose their nerve late in the game. When they do, players will turn on each other and try to protect themselves from criticism. The minute that happens, you have people working against their own best interests.

decision-making process, coaches and players alike, until the decision is made. Others must know who is in command, but a head coach must behave democratically. Then, once a decision is made, the team must be motivated to go ahead and execute it.

What does it take to create a decision-making process in which people feel they can participate?

It starts with the expectations the head coach sets. It is part of the job to expect everyone in the organization to be an expert in his or her particular area of responsibility, to refine their skills continually, and to be physically and intellectually committed to the team. The head coach has to make it clear that he expects everyone to participate and volunteer his or her thoughts, impressions, and ideas. The goal is to create a communication channel that allows important information to get from the bottom to the top.

During 49ers games, my coaches and I always tried to respond to what the players said. We knew that we needed their input. And it often made a difference. For example, in a game against New Orleans in 1987, I told the team at halftime that we would call one particular pass play when we got inside the Saints 30-yard line. In the stress of the moment, when we got there, I simply didn't think of sending in the play. But on the sideline, Steve Young, our backup quarterback, immediately reminded me of it. He wasn't a bit hesitant. I called it, and we scored. I couldn't worry about being embarrassed because I had forgotten what I said in the locker room. We were after results. We all wanted to win.

If that is what it takes to be a successful coach, what are the qualities that define the modern football player?

The key to being a modern football player is the ability to respond quicker, both mentally and physically, than the other player. Some people are naturally quicker physically. But to win, you need to be quicker as a team. You must beat your opposition to the punch every time.

Physical strength and speed are important advantages, but even more advantageous is having the training that permits you to respond intelligently to whatever confronts you. That means more precision, better execution, and quicker response than

ON ORGANIZED LABOR

I've always believed there should be a football players' association. But sometimes the association has worked against the best interests of the rank and file. That was the story of the 1983 NFL players strike. There were certain players' needs that should have been addressed and were not. Things like their safety, medical services, and the condition of the fields. But the union didn't think these things were important. It was just pure dollars to them. It was an example of the players being led by and obligated to follow people who didn't understand the important issues.

Players rely heavily on the business advice of agents and lawyers—often these advisers run every aspect of the players' lives. And sometimes the players accept the judgments of people who take advantage of their emotions and suspicions.

I suppose it's not so surprising that there are even some union leaders in professional sports who use the union as a way to fulfill their own needs at the expense of the members. But even though a strike might be misdirected, it would be a terrible mistake to underestimate the power that is inherent in people grouping together. The players develop a tremendous loyalty to each other, and that bonding won't let them cave in to the owners.

During the 1983 strike, the 49ers did one of the best jobs in the NFL of working around the strike and healing the team afterwards. When you face an issue like a strike, you have to be sensitive without demonstrating weaknesses or vacillating. I didn't lose communication with the striking players. I had empathy for them, and I wasn't confrontational. I was willing to do whatever it took to keep the team together. And although I felt the union leadership was wrong, I understood that the players were obligated to follow it.

your opponents. Under the extreme stress of game conditions, a player must condense his intellect and focus it on thinking more quickly and clearly than the opposition.

How do you achieve that quickness and responsiveness in your teams?

It is all in the way you prepare. Preparation allows us to overcome the fact that we might not be the most physically talented team. During the 1980s, the 49ers may not have been as talented as the New York Giants or Chicago Bears, who had measurable advantages in speed or strength. But we were able to compensate in the way we prepared for a game.

Some coaches rely on relatively simplistic plans. When their plans don't work, they say that it was the players who did not block hard enough, did not run hard enough, or just were not tough enough. We have gone beyond that pattern of failure and finger pointing. The responsibility for the success of the team starts with the coach, who develops the plan that is then executed by the players—who are extremely well-prepared.

Being prepared starts with identifying the essential skills our team needs to compete effectively. The next step is to create a format to teach those skills. Here at Stanford, our practices and game plans are far more detailed than those used by most of our opponents. There is more to learn with our schemes, so we demand more mental commitment and concentration from the players.

How do you approach the job of structuring practices so your players will be prepared?

I believe in extremely precise, minute-by-minute, tightly structured practices. We focus far more intellect and put far more thought into what we do in practice than other teams do. We have five or six skills or techniques that we want each of our players to be able to use in carrying out his assignment, where our opponents usually will have only one or two.

Take an offensive lineman, for example. Before the ball is snapped, that guard or tackle might have only three or four seconds to decide what kind of blocking technique to use on the man in front of him. Say there are four blocking techniques he can use. By the way his man is positioned, by the situation in the game, by what he has learned to expect from his opponent, he will be able to select one of those techniques.

Many other teams take a more simplistic approach. They teach their players one approach, one technique. Our approach gives our players more dimension. When we are playing powerhouses like Notre Dame, Texas A&M, or Washington, we have to use our extra dimensions to compensate for being physically out-manned. That is the intellectual part of the game. That is the area in which we ask more of our players than our opponents are asking of theirs.

How do you teach those skills?

The most important tool for getting things done is the drill. For example, we work on drills to teach running backs about pass protection against blitzing linebackers. You have to identify the six different situations that can occur. Then you have to allocate the time to work on those six situations and also the 20 techniques that you want your running backs to be able to apply. In teaching those skills, sometimes you want to have your guards and tight ends participate, or even the entire offensive unit. All of that requires preparation, discipline, and focus from both coaches and players.

The way I coach, I know ahead of time how I am going to run the whole season's worth of practices. I have established the priorities for what we need to accomplish and allocated the time in which to teach the necessary skills.

I establish the program long before we take the field so I can use most efficiently the time available for learning and so the players do not get bored or distracted. The players must know clearly and at all times exactly what it is that they have to get out of any given drill. After 35 years of coaching, I have found that you can't do anything in less than 10 minutes or in more than 20 minutes.

Another distinction in drills is between those skills and techniques that can be taught individually and those that require groups. It is also critical to allocate time for team play and to build in practice segments that focus on the execution of particular plays and particular game situations that you want to be ready for.

Why is it important to prepare so many skills for so many contingencies?

Making judgments under severe stress is the most difficult thing there is. The more preparation you have prior to the conflict, the more you can do in a clinical situation, the better off you will be. For that reason, in practice I want to make certain that we have accounted for every critical situation, including the desperate ones at the end of a game when we may have only one chance to pull out a victory. Even in that circumstance, I want us to have a play prepared and rehearsed. Say it is the last 20 seconds of a game and we're losing. We have already practiced six plays that we can apply in that situation. That way, we know what to do, and we can calmly execute the plays. We'll have no doubt in our minds, we will have more poise, and we can concentrate without falling prey to desperation.

Can you recall a specific instance where this actually paid off for one of your teams?

In 1987, we were down 26-20 against Cincinnati. We got the ball back on their 25-yard line with two seconds left in the game. It could have been a hopeless situation. We put three receivers to the left and Jerry Rice to the right. Joe Montana got the ball, looked left, pump-faked, and then threw right, where Rice was covered man-to-man in the end zone. It was a touchdown, and it won an important game for us. But it would not have happened if we had not been prepared.

You need to have a plan even for the worst scenario. It doesn't mean that it will always work; it doesn't mean that you will always be successful. But you will always be prepared and at your best.

But the same applies to virtually every situation at every point in the game. Say you are on the defense and inside your own 25-yard line. The situation can vary, so there are a number of particulars you need to prepare for. You have third down and inches. Third down and feet. Third down and yards. Inside the 15-yard line, all that changes, and inside the 5 it changes again. Each situation is different, and for each you might have 15 different game situations to practice. You have to allocate time for all of them, you have to practice plays, and you have to work with individuals. And then all of the separate situations have to be pulled together to give a continuity to the team's play.

One of the most impressive attributes of your 49ers teams was their ability to take what some people might consider a disadvantage and use it to their advantage. Did you work on developing this skill?

I can think of several cases where we consciously tried to work on the players to reverse what in football are usually crippling disadvantages. One was playing on the road. In football, the home-field advantage is often decisive. But we were able to bond together, play in enemy territory, and feed on the emotions of the situation, without being intimidated by the other teams or their fans.

To accomplish that, I would condition the 49ers to adversity. We would talk about how it feels to fly into enemy territory. We would discuss what crosses your mind when you take the field. It allowed us to turn our status as outsiders into our advantage. When I talked with the team, I would use examples from the early days of World War II as illustrations of the desperate and heroic fights we could emulate. By talking about what could be a disadvantage, we turned our people on. We made it an advantage.

The other example is the injury factor. Some teams come unraveled when a star player gets injured. With the 49ers, an injury often served to arouse the team to play harder. Again, my approach was to talk about it openly. I would make the point that reserve players always had to be prepared, and that when they got the chance, they should actually improve on the performance of the injured player. Again, I used historical examples from warfare. For instance, in the Civil War, the best trained people, the front line and even generals, were often the first to fall. Often it was the reserves who would achieve victory. So when our reserves took the field, they were conditioned to feel this way and they knew what was expected. They would feel much more positive about going into the game.

In teaching skills to your players, how do you organize your own thinking about the players you are trying to reach?

Take a group of ten players. The top two will be super-motivated. Superstars will usually take care of themselves. Anybody can coach them. The next four, with the right motivation and direction, will learn to perform up to their potential. The next two will be marginal. With constant attention, they will be able to accomplish something of value to the team. The last two will waste your time. They won't be with you for long. Our goal is to focus our organizational detail and coaching on the middle six. They are the ones who most need and benefit from your direction, monitoring, and counsel.

How do you achieve a balance between group skills and discipline on the one hand and player individuality on the other?

They go together in defining the two directions you need to pursue at the same time. First, you develop within the organization and the players an appreciation for the role each athlete plays on the team. You talk to each player and let each one know that, at some point, he will be in a position to win or lose a game. It may be one play in an entire career for a certain player or many plays each game for a Joe Montana. But the point is that everyone's job is essential. Everyone has a specific role and specific responsibilities. And each player has to be prepared both mentally and physically to the utmost to play that role.

Second, you talk to each player and indicate the importance of everyone's participation in the process—that it is important for everyone to express himself, to offer ideas, explanations, solutions, formulas. You want everyone to enter into the flow of ideas, even ideas that may seem extreme in their creativity.

You are actually striving for two things at the same time: an organization where people understand the importance of their jobs and are committed to living within the confines of those jobs and to taking direction; and an organization where people feel creative and adaptive and are willing to change their minds without feeling threatened. It is a tough combination to achieve. But it's also the ultimate in management.

Is there a situation with a player that exemplifies this balance between giving explicit direction and permitting individual creativity?

Take Joe Montana, for example. He is a perfect combination of the two vital aspects that are necessary for developing greatness as a quarterback.

The formula for the success of the 49ers offense was a highly disciplined, very structured form of utilizing the forward pass. To make our system work, Joe had to master the disciplines to know which receiver to throw to, when, and why. The success of the team depended on Joe's ability to work within that framework. Consequently, the job of the coach was to use drills and repetition so that Joe developed almost automatic moves and decision-making ability.

But there is an extra quality that it takes for a quarterback to become a world champion—or, in Joe's case, the best ever. And that is an instinctive, spontaneous, natural response to situations that arise in games. Part of Montana's greatness was that 10% to 15% of the time his spontaneous instincts would break loose and make a phenomenal difference in the outcome of a game.

It is the job of the coach to find the best of both sides. We had to have a very structured system of football, and we also wanted instinctive and spontaneous play.

How do you go about the job of coaching a player like Montana to develop that kind of balance?

Early on, we had to encourage Joe to trust his spontaneous instincts. We were careful not to criticize him when he used his creative abilities and things did not work out. In practice, we worked with Joe repeatedly on specific plays. When he was placed in a game, we called only those plays because we knew that he should be confident that he could execute them. But we didn't jump him the minute he would break the pattern. Instead, we nurtured him to use his instincts. We had to allow him to be wrong on occasion and to live with it.

Of course, with different players the problem takes on a different look. In the case of quarterback Steve Young, it was almost the opposite. We had to work with him to be disciplined enough to live within the strict framework of what we were doing. Steve is a great spontaneous athlete and a terrific runner. But we found that we had to reduce the number of times he would use his instincts and increase his willingness to stay within the confines of the team concept.

For example, we would be at a point in a game where we had designed a special play to break the defense wide open and score a touchdown. In his early days, Steve might not have had the discipline to wait for that play to develop. Instead, he would see an opening and run with the ball for a five-yard gain. He would let his instincts and emotions affect his patience with the play and his confidence that the entire team could execute.

COLLEGE FOOTBALL: THE PROFESSIONAL APPROACH

Part of the agreement that brought Bill Walsh back to Stanford in 1992 was that he be allowed to pick his assistant coaches. Of the nine assistants, one, Fred von Appen, is a former 49ers coach, and four, Bill Ring, Mike Wilson, Tom Holmoe, and Keena Turner, are former 49ers players. Turner, an outside linebacker who played on all four 49ers Super Bowl championship teams, was known as a "player's leader." As Walsh puts it, "Keena's inner strength and quiet, unobtrusive leadership most exemplified the 49ers personality."

Walsh's respect for players continues at Stanford, where, according to Turner, one of Walsh's greatest strengths is his ability to encourage communication and a sense of affinity among the players. "Coach Walsh is not an authority figure bellowing out commands," Turner insists. "Instead, he promotes closeness. One of the primary concerns that Bill passes on to his assistants is that we never demean a player, that we don't even holler. We must coach in a way that is respectful."

But during the first few months of Stanford practices, Turner was also made aware that the mythology and expectations that had been building up around Walsh could be as misleading and detrimental as they were potentially animating. "Where people get lost concerning Bill is that 'genius' label he has been saddled with. It's not always true that Bill's way is the only way that works, and he knows that too. And I don't want to paint him like a saint. He encourages the assistants to respect the players, but it's not as if he's never gone off on a guy." One factor that continues to amaze Turner is Walsh's organizing scheme. "Bill has a plan for everything. For example, take our game at Notre Dame last October. At halftime, we were down by 16 points, and I'm sure everyone watching had written us off. But in the locker room, there was no sense of panic. We had a calm, thoughtful discussion on how to get it done. The players handled it because Bill had laid the groundwork. He had prepared us to be 16 points down. All he had to ask was, 'Do you pack it up or figure out how to win?'" The response was decidedly the latter. In the second half, a determined Stanford team, quite reminiscent of the Walsh 49ers, marched on the field and methodically crushed Notre Dame 33 to 16.

As a coach, how do you know what it takes to bring out the best in a young player's abilities?

Unfortunately, there is nothing exact about it. Experience is really the only teacher. I was 47 years old when I became an NFL head coach. Typically, that job comes to people when they are between the ages of 35 and 40. I was in a subordinate role as an assistant coach for a longer period of time than most, so I was forced to analyze, evaluate, and learn to appreciate the roles that other people play more than I might have. In retrospect, I was lucky.

But if developing your players is an inexact art, there are bound to be mistakes. How do you deal with them?

Again and again in the development and selection of personnel, you have to account for miscalculation. In professional sports, the person who is best at dealing with personnel is the person who recognizes his or her errors and deals with them the quickest and most effectively. That could mean adopting a long-term approach, or it could mean the release of a player.

Take our drafting of John Taylor in 1986. John came to the 49ers as a wide receiver from Delaware State. He had great physical talent, but not a lot of background in playing sophisticated football. We simply miscalculated how long it would take John to be ready to play in the NFL. Consequently, we were disappointed in him. John was not adapting well to the competition, he appeared confused and frustrated, and he had lost his enthusiasm.

But instead of giving up on him, we took a longer term, more patient approach. We waited an extra year to allow him to mature and grow into this level of competition and into the role we wanted him to play. Now, he is an All-Pro and one of the great receivers in the game.

The other side to that would be the decision I made with Thomas "Hollywood" Henderson. He was a very bright, articulate, charming person, but he also had an uncontrollable drug habit. I made a calculated choice that involved a high risk when we acquired him from Dallas—that I could personally nurture and rehab and influence Thomas into once again becoming a great linebacker. It was a miscalculation on my part. I gave it every chance to work, but finally I had to decide that it simply was not going to.

When you reach that point, you have to make a controlled and well-planned retreat. You regret the decision that you made, but you have to live with it, and you have to work yourself out of it. That is one important facet of good management: deciding how to acknowledge your mistakes.

Do you simply gloss over them? Do you blame someone else? Are you so insecure that your ego will not let you do anything but maintain that your original decision was correct? I could have kept Thomas Henderson on the team, but then the 49ers would not have become world champs. Or I could have had the public blaming Thomas or blaming an assistant coach. But none of those approaches would have helped the team.

In this case, I did not want to publicly embarrass Thomas, but I did want to show the team that I was still in control and that drug abuse would not be tolerated. We simply had to move as smoothly as possible to release Thomas for any number of reasons, remove him from the picture. I made a mistake, acknowledged it, and decided what to do about it.

If the personnel issue is so overriding, do you have a methodology for the way you evaluate players?

We use a five-bracket ranking system to categorize people we are looking at. The first is the star player who cannot miss. The second is a player who will someday be a starter and play for a number of years. The third will make the team, and the fourth has an isolated specialty—covering kickoffs or fielding punts. The fifth is someone who will make the squad and help you by playing solidly in a backup role.

You want as many superstars as you can get. The more stars, the better. But the difference between winning and losing is the bottom 25% of your people. Most coaches can deliver the top 75%. But the last 25% only blossoms in the details, in the orchestration of skills, in the way you prepare.

When you go into a draft, what are the particulars you are looking for in a player?

It is always a combination of factors that add up to the right person. It's his level of natural ability. It's his competitive instincts. It's also the history of that athlete; his ability to learn, retain, and apply what he has learned; and his ability to work under stress with other people.

Then you have to be able to project those qualities into the slot or role that athlete would play for your team. And you have to do that over time, thinking about the short, middle, and long term. For example, a player could come in and play a certain role in his first year, and then in his second year that role could develop or be enhanced. After a number of years, that player might end up in a feature role, and then revert back to the role in which he started as the wear and tear of the game begins to take its toll.

You have said that one of the most important attributes of any organization is the way it treats its people. In pro football, with frequent trading and the yearly competition from rookies for veterans' jobs, cutting a veteran player or convincing him to retire is a big part of your job. How do you handle that part of the personnel issue?

Any good coach or manager has got to be responsible for phasing his people through the organization. It may be the most emotionally difficult part of the job. When you do it, you often end up as the most unpopular person in the organization. Yet it is part of the role that the leader must play. It has to be done and done continually. You have to be prepared to use your own professional judgment as to when and why it is time for one of your players to call it quits.

As the head coach, I forced myself to deal with this process rather than turn my back on it or hand it off to the assistant coaches. In fact, in this area you can only listen to the assistant coaches so much because, typically, they would rather have veteran players on the team. It makes their coaching job easier. Subconsciously, I think assistant coaches feel much more comfortable with ten-year players than with the rookies. The coaches have become friends with the veterans, they have great faith in them, they understand each other. And the veterans already know what the coaches want done out on the field.

In sports, there is an arc of utilization that describes most athletes' careers. By that I mean a curve that a coach can use to project what a player can do now, next year, and ten years from now. A player may be a superstar this year, but with minor injuries nicking at him and starting to add up, he won't be a superstar three years from now. And then in the next phase you have to begin thinking about replacing him.

Most people don't realize it, but the players who get all the attention are usually the ones on the downside of their careers. Ironically, the organization is often paying the most money to the team members who are on the descending curve as players. When players are starting to wind down their careers but are still playing effectively, you have to remind yourself how to use them. You have to gauge how they practice, what you ask them to do on the field, what kinds of situations you use them in, how much playing time they get. These are all factors that ultimately lead to the point where you judge that a younger player could do the job as well. That younger player is on an ascending curve on the arc. That is when you have to make your move.

How do you go about making that move without dealing the veteran player a crushing blow?

There will be some suffering, and there is no way to avoid it. It's simply part of the process. There will be agonizing, frustration, and anger. But the coach has to make the decision to improve the team. The real danger is if the decision aimed at improving the team leads to so much bitterness that the fallout causes other players to take sides. When the team becomes divided, the decision has done more harm than good.

That is why managing people's emotions is such an important part of the coach's job. You begin by acknowledging that your decision will cause some suffering. Then you do whatever you can to soften the edges, to reduce the anguish and frustration, to communicate your own sensitivity, and, in a sense, even to manipulate the player.

You recommend manipulating people rather than being honest?

The easiest thing is to be truly honest and direct. In fact, it sounds just great to say that you are going to be honest and direct. But insensitive, hammer-like shots that are delivered in the name of honesty and openness usually do the greatest damage to people. The damage ends up reverberating throughout the entire organization. Over time, people will lose the bonding factor they need for success. And over time, that directness will isolate you from the people with whom you work.

The real task is to lead people through the troubled times, when they are demoted or find themselves at the end of their playing days, and to help them maintain as much of their self-esteem as possible. These are the tasks that really define the job of the manager. A manager's job is not simply having a desk filled with family pictures and a wall covered by plaques for good behavior. It's developing the skills to understand and deal with people.

You have described a variety of tasks that the coach has to be sensitive to, including the ability to make tough decisions and the need to soften the edges when it comes to dealing with people. What has made your system so successful?

The bottom line in professional sports is winning. Everything has to focus on that product: winning football games. Other offshoots—the public relations, the merchandising, the high-sounding philosophical approach—mean little compared with being successful on the playing field.

But winning does not necessarily mean being a victor in every game. It's not winning every game at any cost. We have to remind ourselves that it's not just a single game that we are trying to win. It is a season and a series of seasons in which the team wins more games than it loses and each team member plays up to his potential. If you are continually developing your skills and refining your approach, then winning will be the final result.

But I have seen coaches who are simply too sentimental, who allow themselves to be too maudlin about "breaking up the old family." They are going to lose sight of the bottom line. And there is another kind who are severe, tough, and hard-hitting. But they sacrifice the loyalty of the people around them. In that situation, people are always afraid that they are going to be the next to go. These coaches rarely have sustained success.

Somewhere in the middle are the coaches who know that the job is to win, who know that they must be decisive, that they must phase people through their organizations, and at the same time they are sensitive to the feelings, loyalties, and emotions that people have toward one another. If you don't have these feelings, I do not know how you can lead anyone.

I have spent many sleepless nights trying to figure out how I was going to phase out certain players for whom I had a strong feelings, but that was my job. I wasn't hired to do anything but win.

PERICLES OF ATHENS—DRAWING FROM THE ESSENCE OF STRATEGIC LEADERSHIP

STEPHEN CUMMINGS

Most of those in the business of developing corporate strategy have at best only a vague understanding of the origins and history of their occupation. By contrast, those pursuing careers in fields such as law, economics, medicine, engineering, and architecture are, through their study and apprenticeship, imbued with a sense of their roots and traditions, from which they draw a great deal of pride, inspiration, and focus. Those in the professions carry within them a great sense of the history of their disciplines. Those whose role it is to combine these fields to best advantage are not.

Corporate strategists in the Eastern world draw inspiration through history from Sun Tzu's *The Art of War*, a treatise on military strategy written in China in the fourth century B.C.

In recognition of the efficacy of this work, *The Art of War* is increasingly read and lauded by Western business people today. But though this interest is well-founded, there also exists a Western tradition of similar value, one which was emerging in ancient Greece around the same time that Sun Tzu was writing.

It is not surprising that this has not been widely recognized. Although the Chinese were exceptionally good at preserving libraries, the Mediterranean peoples were quite good at destroying them. Sun Tzu's work has been handed down to us complete, but there remain only scattered, and often piecemeal, sources that inform us of ancient Greek strategic practice and thought. This article seeks to unearth some of this rich and inspirational history by describing the life and times of Pericles, widely regarded as the greatest strategist in classical Greece and leader of Athens during its Golden Age—an age acknowledged as the birth of Western civilization.

No better argument for undertaking such an excursion into history could be provided than that of Plutarch, biographer of the classical world's great leaders. On the importance of new generations studying the great leaders of the past he says:

> It is true, of course, that our outward sense cannot avoid apprehending the various objects it encounters, merely by virtue of their impact and regardless of whether they are useful or not; but a man's conscious intellect is something which he may bring to bear or avert as he chooses, and can very easily transfer it to another object as he sees fit. For this reason we ought to seek out virtue not merely to contemplate it, but to derive benefit from doing so. A color, for example, is well suited to the eye if its bright and agreeable tones stimulate and refresh the vision; and in the same way we ought to apply our intellectual vision to those models which can inspire it to attain its own proper virtue through the sense of delight they arouse. [Such a model is] no sooner

seen than it rouses the spectator to action, and yet it does not form his character by mere imitation, but by promoting the understanding of virtuous deeds it provides him with a dominating purpose. (Plutarch, *Life of Pericles*)

This article outlines the Western origins of strategy, the emergence of the role of the strategist, Pericles' conception of strategy, the manner of his strategic leadership, and his approach to implementation. Times have changed, and Pericles' ideas should not be imitated as a "formula for success" today. Rather, the story of Pericles' interpretation of strategic leadership, set against classical perceptions of strategy and the role of the strategist, can stimulate and refresh the vision, inspiring and focusing the energies of those concerned with corporate strategy and leadership today.

THE ORIGIN OF STRATEGY

The word "strategy" derives from the ancient Athenian title *strategos*, denoting a supreme commander of the Athenian armed forces. The position was created as part of Cleisthenes' sociopolitical reforms of Athens instigated in 508 B.C. and combined the words *stratos* ("army") and *agein* ("to lead"). Cleisthenes' reforms saw the creation of ten new tribal divisions that acted as both military and political subunits of the district of Athens. Each tribe was headed by a strategos for which elections were held each year. Collectively, the ten incumbent strategoi formed the Athenian war council which, because of the kudos granted it, greatly influenced civilian as well as military affairs.

The creation of the position of strategos reflected increasing military decision-making complexity. Warfare had evolved to the point at which winning sides relied no longer on the deeds of heroic individuals, but on the coordination of many different units of men fighting in close formation. This, combined with the increasing significance of naval forces, mercenaries, and military/political alliances, multiplied considerably the variables commanders had to consider when planning actions, pushing questions of coordination and synergy to the forefront of decision making.

THE EMERGENCE OF THE ROLE OF THE STRATEGIST

If what you thirst for is repute and admiration, try to make sure of one accomplishment: that is to know the business which you propose to carry out.

—Xenophon, *Memorabilia*

The ancients believed strategy to be very much a leadership task—what we today might term a "line" function. Aineias the Tactician, author of the earliest surviving Western volume devoted to military strategy (*How to Survive Under Siege*, written in the mid-fourth century B.C.), was primarily concerned with how leaders should deploy available manpower and other resources to best advantage. The Roman Frontinus expands this definition to encompass "everything achieved by a commander, be it characterized by foresight, advantage, enterprise, or resolution."

As the primary elected officials and power brokers in Athenian society, strategoi were expected to be the wisest of citizens. A belief that the measure of one's wisdom was one's ability to combine political acumen and practical intelligence meant that the Athenians demanded that their strategoi function with an awareness of how things worked at the "front line."

To be considered a credible candidate for the position of strategos one had to have demonstrated prowess in both individual combat and "hands-on" military leadership. This prerequisite for hands-on leadership incorporated the belief that strategoi should be present in the thick of battle, not merely direct their forces from afar. It was felt that the front line was often the best place for the strategos to read the mood of the battlefield, implementing and adapting plans as events unfolded, engendering a feeling of commitment and respect that only fighting elbow to elbow with his fellow citizens could promote.

Although success was, to a large extent, in the hands of the strategoi, the relationship between society and strategist was reciprocal. Strategoi had to demonstrate a willingness to share burdens: "No man was considered fit to give fair and honest advice in council if he had not, like his fellows, a family at stake in the hour of the city's danger" (Thucydides). The strategic leadership of the Athenian organization was not to consider itself immune from the hardships suffered by other members of society when times were tough.

The structure of the Athenian sociopolitical organization designed by Cleisthenes enabled the development of such practical, "hands-on" strategists. Cleisthenes' design was highly recursive. The new tribes, and the local communities these tribes comprised, formed the units and subunits of the army and were, in their sociopolitical structures, tantamount to the city state in microcosm. Decision makers at all levels were expected to think strategically on issues related to their local concerns, and these subunits proved an excellent training ground for the type of strategos outlined above. A man who knew the workings of his local organization would not be lost in affairs concerning the society as a whole.

Strategy was perceived by the originators of the term as a leadership task and a line function. By contrast, many companies in the modern era have viewed their "strategic planning units" as advisory or staff functions, called in to tackle specific projects but somewhat removed from the action themselves (Mintzberg, 1994). The Athenians placed the onus for strategic thinking squarely on the shoulders of their leaders, believing that these leader-strategists could not function effectively without structures and systems in place that promoted an appreciation of the way things worked where the "work" was done.

PERICLES OUTLINES THE ESSENCE OF STRATEGY

To know what must be done and be able to explain it ....

—Pericles

Cleisthenes' Athenian system reached its zenith under Pericles. Repeatedly elected strategos from the mid-fifth century B.C., and considered the leader of the council of strategoi for much of this period until his death in 429 B.C., Pericles directed Athens through a golden age. An examination of Pericles' attitude toward his role as strategos reveals a simple yet powerful articulation of what strategy boils down to. The leader-strategist's primary tasks are to have a vision and effectively articulate and communicate it. Pericles, in a speech reported by Thucydides, promoted himself to the people of Athens as "one who has at least as much ability as anyone else to see what ought to be done and explain what he sees." He went on to say that "a man who has the knowledge but lacks the power clearly to express it is no better off than if he never had any ideas at all."

Pericles' vision is perhaps best summed up in Thucydides' interpretation of his funeral oration in the first year of the Second Peloponnesian War with Sparta. In a manner not uncommon in successful corporations today, Pericles invoked the memories of the founders and developers of the Athenian organization as a means of motivating like-minded actions in the future. To paraphrase, Pericles' vision was of Athens as a liberal city in contrast to its rivals, unique in its system of government, military training methods, and approach to schooling. Athenians should strive to be superior to their competitors in their independence of spirit, manysidedness of attainment, and self-reliance. To achieve this they must be, as they had always been, reflective yet adventurous. Interestingly, this speech, often revered as one of the greatest pieces of political oratory, has recently been claimed by Clemens and Mayer (1987) to be one of the finest statements of an organization's shared values and beliefs. Pericles' vision focused the energies of his fellow Athenians by encapsulating what they were striving to maintain, renew, and promote—their uniqueness, their culture.

Pericles was particularly effective in conveying his vision to his fellow citizens. It was said that whenever he stood up "he spoke right past the politicians, from ten feet behind, like a great sprinter" (Eupolis, Demoi, from Rusten 1989). At the same time, Pericles was extremely cautious in his use of words. He recognized that rhetoric was the art of working on the souls of men by means of words. As such it required an adroit knowledge of men's characters and passions and a most skillful and delicate touch. Whenever Pericles rose to speak he uttered a prayer that no word might escape his lips that was unsuited to the matter at hand, and he was careful not to speak on every question, reserving himself for occasions he believed to be of particular importance. This helped create what Eupolis, a fellow Athenian, termed a "credibility on his lips which left a sting in his hearers." To an Athenian's way of thinking it was restraint that, of all manifestations of power, impressed most of all.

Historian H. Delbruck (1975) suggests that the most striking proof of Pericles' greatness lay in his ability to persuade the sovereign Athenian citizenry to adopt strategies that seemed so hard to grasp. Kagan (1991) lauds his knack for explaining how the interests of the corporate city and its citizens depended on each other for its fulfillment. Pericles' achievements tell us that successful strategic leaders must draw a corporate vision from that which makes their organizations different, and empower their supporters by communicating that vision in a manner that provides a focal point for their energies.

PERICLES' APPROACH TO THE IMPLEMENTATION OF STRATEGY

To face calamity with a mind as unclouded as may be, and quickly to react against it—that, in a city and in an individual, is real strength.

—Thucydides

Renowned for his wariness and generally a methodical man, Pericles had a goal for his military strategies that Kagan (1991) describes as limiting risk while holding fast to essential points and principles. Pragmatic in his realization that victory came from intelligent resolution and financial resources, and cool-headed enough to urge his fellow Athenians not to take their "eyes off the ball" by undertaking too many new conquests during a war, Pericles nevertheless demonstrated an unpredictability that kept his rivals on their toes. Frontinus tells the tale of one such ruse:

> Pericles' men, being driven by the Peloponnesians into a place surrounded on all sides by precipitous cliffs and provided with only two outlets, dug a ditch of great breadth on one side as if to shut it off from the enemy; on the other side he began to build a road, as if intending to make a sally by this. The besiegers, not supposing that Pericles' army would make its escape by the ditch which he constructed, massed to oppose him on the side where the road was. But Pericles, spanning the ditch by bridges which he had made already, extricated his men without interference.

Not unlike many recent strategic theorists, the Athenians appreciated timing and speed of implementation as sources of competitive advantage. The Athenians were praised by Thucydides as "men who were capable of real action, first making their plans and then going forward without hesitation while their enemies had still not made up their minds." The key to greatness of Themistocles, the leading strategos during the Greeks' war with Xerxes' Persians, was said to be his ability to "do precisely the right thing at precisely the right moment."

Pericles' concern for ensuring that thought was given to the timing of implementation is described by Plutarch:

> Pericles found Tolmides, a soldier who had previously enjoyed particularly good fortune and had had exceptional honors bestowed upon him for his campaigns, preparing to invade Boeotia. Tolmides had given no thought to the right moment for launching the attack, but he had persuaded 1,000 of the bravest and most adventurous men of military age to volunteer. Pericles did his utmost in the Assembly to restrain Tolmides and dissuade him from going, and he remarked in a famous phrase that if he would not listen to Pericles he would be wise to be guided by time, the most experienced counselor of all. This saying did not bring him much credit at that moment. But a few days afterward the news came that Tolmides had been defeated and killed in a battle near Coronea and that many of the bravest Athenians had fallen with him, and this greatly increased the admiration and goodwill the people felt toward Pericles, since he now seemed to them a man of foresight as well as a patriot.

Pericles' reputation as a cautious general should not obscure his own daring and courage in battle. Plutarch notes that he was, on occasion, "the most conspicuous of all in taking no care for his safety." Despite his conservative nature,

Pericles recognized that competition creates crucial situations that must be exploited with bold courage, and he was famous for the maxim "opportunity waits for no man." The strategist must balance the risk of acting before situations can be properly assessed and forces mobilized, with the knowledge that being the prime mover can be a tremendous strategic advantage. One must be reflective yet adventurous.

At first, Pericles' approach to strategic development appears incoherent, methodical yet unpredictable, cautious yet daring. However, on further reflection it demonstrates an astute understanding of the paradoxical nature of strategy. Though commended for having a systematic approach to implementation and an appreciation for detail, Pericles accepted the futility of religiously adhering to detailed plans, knowing that goals made in advance of events are unlikely to be realized exactly. Said Thucydides, "No one can alike conceive and dare in the same spirit of confidence." He noted that Pericles maintained, "There is often no more logic in the course of events than there is in the plans of men; this is why we blame our luck when things happen in ways that we did not expect." Rational planning preceding action is a sensible and worthy aim, but there is a danger in treating plans as inviolable. Religious adherence to plans may stifle the potential gains provided by the sort of opportunistic creativity that can only occur as events develop.

As described earlier, the Athenians were concerned that their strategoi involve themselves at the front so they could read events as they occurred and be well placed to adjust their plans accordingly as the battle unfolded. It seems they understood well what Western theorists in the modern age are only just now beginning to understand: Though it may pay to have a plan, the art of the strategist is as much about effectively improvising and changing plans as it is about making them. The art of strategy formulation and implementation requires an ability to anticipate and plan as a means of providing impetus, and, just as important, an ability to effectively react to unforeseen problems and opportunities.

The original conception of the strategist's position reflected increasing military decision-making complexity. Successful organizations no longer depended on the deeds of heroic individuals, but on the coordination of many different units. This pushed questions of coordination and synergy to the forefront of decision-making.

The ancient Athenians believed that strategy was the primary responsibility of the leaders of their society, and that those strategist-leaders, to be effective, must have an understanding of the way things worked at the front line. Good strategist-leaders must be seen to be facing risks as great as if not greater than those whom they expect to follow them. Strategoi were expected to lead from the front for this reason, and because the front line was often the best place to read the mood of a battle and enact a change of plans should unforeseen opportunities or problems present themselves.

Good strategist-leaders have two primary attributes: an ability to see what must be done and an ability to communicate it. They must be able to construct an inspiring vision, but this in itself is of little use if it is not then articulated and communicated in such a way as to inspire, and provide a focal point for, the members of the corporation. A good sense of timing is crucial as well. Strategist-leaders must paradoxically be reflective yet adventurous; they must have good plans prepared but at the same time be ready to forgo those plans.

Tsoukas (1991) holds that strategos—the progenitor of strategist—has become a "dead metaphor," no longer associated with its progeny. The present lack of interest in the genealogical roots of strategy, which this article seeks to rectify, is due to a combination of indifference—likely caused by the fact that most strategists graduate to this role after an emergence in a field already well endowed with history—and misunderstanding about the modus operandi of great ancient strategists like Pericles.

Henry Mintzberg (1987), in an article describing what he believes (with good reason) to be the true nature of strategy, appears to bemoan strategy's Greek military origins as misleading people in their understanding of strategy and detrimental to a recognition that strategy is a "craft." Ironically, the ancient Athenian's beliefs seem remarkably similar to those of Mintzberg. It is not so much that the ways of strategoi are not relevant to modern strategic practice, but that most peoples' understanding of Greek society and military practice is imbued with notions of the "detached" nature of more modern military strategic development. Strategy was viewed as a craft by the ancients much as it is by "enlightened" modern management gurus today.

It is suggested here that our conception of strategy in the Western industrial age, with its focus on strategists as distant yet omniscient rational planners offering incontrovertible advice to leaders too busy to concern themselves with strategy, is an anomaly. Modern management "science" is only now waking up to what earlier societies, such as ancient Athens, understood well. The dissemination of an awareness of strategy's meaning at its conception should help speed this reawakening.

Xenophon describes the ideal strategist-leader as "ingenious, energetic, careful, full of stamina and presence of mind, loving and tough, straightforward and crafty, alert and deceptive, ready to gamble everything and wishing to have everything, generous and greedy, trusting and suspicious." Of all the leaders of his age, Pericles best satisfied this description. At his death he considered his highest claim to honor to be that, despite the immense power he wielded, he had never given way to feelings of envy or hatred, and had treated no man as so irreconcilable an enemy that he could never become his friend. In this is contained a final word of wisdom—today's competitors may be tomorrow's allies.

REFERENCES

Clemens, J. and Mayer, D.F. (1987). *The Classic Touch: Lessons in Leadership from Homer to Hemingway.* Homewood, IL: Dow Jones Irwin.

Chen, M. (1994). "Sun Tzu's Strategic Thinking and Contemporary Business," *Business Horizons*, March-April: 42–48.

Cummings, S. and Brocklesby, J. (1993). "The Classical System—Organizational Insights into What Made Periclean Athens Great," *Systems Practice*, 6, 4: 335–357.

Delbruck, H. (1975). *The History of the Art of War—Within the Framework of Political History*, trans. by W. Renfroe Jr. Westport, CT: Greenwood.

Kagan, D. (1991). *Pericles of Athens and the Birth of Democracy.* New York: Free Press.

Mintzberg, H. (1994). "The Fall and Rise of Strategic Planning," *Harvard Business Review*, January-February: 107–114.

Mintzberg, H. (1989). *Mintzberg on Management: Inside Our Strange World of Organizations.* New York: Free Press.

Mintzberg, H. (1987). "Crafting Strategy," *Harvard Business Review*, July-August: 66–75.

Rusten, J.S. (1989). *The Peloponnesian War, Book II.* New York: Cambridge University Press.

Tsoukas, H. (1991). "The Missing Link: A Transformational View of Metaphors in Organizational Science," *Academy of Management Review*, 16, 3: 566–585.

Weick, K.E. (1987). "Substitutes for Strategy," in D.J. Teece (ed.), *The Competitive Challenge: Strategies for Industrial Innovation and Renewal.* Cambridge, MA: Ballinger Publ. Co.: 223–233.

Whitehead, D. (1986). *The Demes of Attica.* Princeton, NJ: Princeton University Press.

Whittington, R. (1992). *What Is Strategy—And Does It Matter?* London: Routledge.

QUESTIONS: SECTION ONE

BASEBALL, FOOTBALL, AND BASKETBALL: MODELS FOR BUSINESS
ROBERT W. KEIDEL

1. What characteristics would a *CEO/strategist* in a baseball-type company need to have? A football-type company? A basketball-type company?

2. What characteristics would the *employees* in a baseball-type company need to have? A football-type company? A basketball-type company?

3. What would happen if a CEO with a football-type mind-set became the leader of a basketball-type company? A baseball-type company?

4. If a company is growing, what sorts of characteristics might be sought in a CEO? Can a leader's mind-set evolve from one model to another over time as an organization grows?

5. Think of other team sports. Using Keidel's dimensions, describe the models for these sports and the types of managers they represent. What sorts of companies do these models describe? What characteristics would a strategist in these types of companies need to have?

6. If a large company wanted to regain innovativeness, what sports model might apply? What sort of sports mind-set would be sought in a CEO?

7. What type of mind-set do you view yourself as having? What sort of organization do you think you would be best suited for as a leader? As an employee?

TO BUILD A WINNING TEAM: AN INTERVIEW WITH HEAD COACH BILL WALSH
RICHARD RAPAPORT

1. What changes has Bill Walsh observed in professional football, which he also believes have occurred in business?

2. How does the "new football" model differ from the football model described by Keidel?

3. What characteristics does Walsh believe a leader of the new football organizations should have? How does this differ from the characteristics of Keidel's football-type leader?

4. How can the new football leader foster two-way communication in the organization?

5. What skills are important in leading a football-type organization?

6. Are there good examples of companies today that reflect the new football-type company? Are there leaders who represent the mind-set of the new football-type leader?

PERICLES OF ATHENS—DRAWING FROM THE ESSENCE OF STRATEGIC LEADERSHIP
STEPHEN CUMMINGS

1. What were the characteristics of the strategos in ancient Greece? What attributes of the socio-political structure made this an appropriate model for strategic leader?

2. What characteristics of Pericles made him an effective strategist?

3. How would you describe Pericles' approach to strategy?

4. Would Pericles be effective as a strategist in a modern company? Why or why not?

2

ALTERNATE ROUTES

Larry has got Buddhas all over his house, but he's not a Buddha. He's a samurai warrior. He's the destroyer, the transformer. It's what he does best.

—Mark Benioff, former Oracle executive, commenting on Oracle CEO Larry Ellison (Hamm, 2000)

"Oh, East is East, and, West is West," wrote Kipling, "and never the twain shall meet." In the business realm, however, these once divergent paths *have* crossed. Western and Eastern firms are partners as well as opponents. "To succeed at global competition," writes Rosalie Tung, author of one of the readings in this section, "we must try to understand ourselves and our overseas counterparts—to judge certain practices and procedures, but also their motivations, morality, and philosophies on cooperating and competing." Metaphors from other cultures help us understand their assumptions and more correctly interpret behavior, and also widen our own repertoire of concepts and ways to communicate.

As a widely read classic in China, Sun Tzu's *The Art of War* gives Westerners insight into Chinese business. Min Chen, the author of the initial article in this section, sees many parallels between this fifth-century B.C. treatise on military strategy and the battlefield of business. Chen also notes differences between Western and Eastern business strategy that can be traced to Sun Tzu. For example, the Chinese place strong emphasis on a leader's moral influence in mobilizing subordinates. The Chinese leader's concern for his underlings borders on familial love, and goes hand in hand with the expectation of unwavering loyalty in return. Chen also credits *The Art of War* with the Chinese tendency to place more of a premium on broad leadership ability when choosing CEOs, as opposed to specialized technical skills.

Sun Tzu is not the only strategist that has influenced modern Asian thinking. Rosalie Tung summarizes lessons on strategy derived from not only *The Art of War*, but three other classic Asian tomes: *The Book of Five Rings*, *The Three Kingdoms*, and *The Thirty-Six Stratagems*. Several of the themes that underlie these works probably sound foreign to Westerners. One is the assumption of the cyclical nature of life, which in Asian culture leads to inevitable ups and downs. Translation: While the fortunes of some Asian countries may have turned downward in the past several years, they will rise again. Deception plays more of a role in strategy in the East. Tung argues that Asian businesspeople are not above creating illusions to gain advantage over an opponent. Neither are they averse to practicing what might be considered in the West as questionable practices in intelligence gathering. It's all just strategy.

In Tung's article, lessons gleaned from the various sources are grouped together. However, she emphasizes that, as common as it is in the West to group many nations under the rubric "Asia," business strategy in China, Korea, and Japan are not alike. Each has some distinctive roots and assumptions, many of which are almost invisible to outsiders, thanks to the high context cultures of Asia. In these countries, Tung reminds us, the meaning of words and actions are deeply intertwined with culture and often cannot be interpreted in the absence of cultural knowledge. It follows that Asians are less inclined to take words and actions at face value, and apt to look for what underlies them.

Eastern strategy also sheds light on the question that arose in the previous section regarding the relevance of metaphors from Western athletics and military to contemporary business strategy. They are still germane. Successful strategists in the East are able to combine many approaches to strategy in a multitude of ways given circumstances, and they willingly accept the inherent contradictions among strategies. Thus, metaphors do not supplant one another: together they comprise a rich arsenal from which business strategists can draw.

SUN TZU'S STRATEGIC THINKING AND CONTEMPORARY BUSINESS

MIN CHEN

The Chinese expression "Shang Chang Ru Zhan Chang" is translated into English as "The marketplace is a battlefield." This is how Asians view success or failure in the business world. From the Asian perspective, the success or failure of a family business directly influences the survival and well-being of the family. The success or failure of a nation's economy affects the survival and well-being of a nation. Therefore, many Asians treat business competition as life-and-death warfare.

Many Western business people, for example, have observed that the Japanese conduct business as if they were waging a war, using the term "waging business" to describe the intensity of Japanese competitive strategies. Because the marketplace, in the eyes of Asians, is a battlefield, military strategy is held to be very useful in guiding business activities. Many Asian business leaders have attached great importance to the classical Chinese military strategies. Many of the principles behind these strategies are even commonly applied to daily life.

MILITARY STRATEGIES AND BUSINESS COMPETITIONS

In Chinese, the word military strategy consists of two parts: *Bing* ("soldier") and *Fa* ("doctrine"), which together can also be translated to mean "the art of war." The golden era in the development of classical Chinese military strategy was the few hundred years between the beginning of the Spring-Autumn period and the end of the Warring States period in Chinese history (772–221 B.C.). Many of the classic strategies were written during this period, because it was a time of constant warfare and of the famous "hundred flowers blooming" and "hundred schools debating." Many of the greatest Chinese philosophers—Confucius, Mencius, Lao Tzu, Zhuang Tzu, and Han Fei Tzu—lived during this period. Their philosophies left an indelible imprint on classical Chinese military strategy.

The *Sun Tzu Bing-Fa*, allegedly written by the master Sun Tzu in the fourth century B.C., is the most complete and reputable book of military strategy that has survived to date. It is still difficult to determine the biography of the author, who supposedly was a subject of Kingdom Qi and a contemporary of Confucius. Around 512 B.C., he traveled to Kingdom Wu and was appointed general. In the ensuing 30 years, he won numerous wars and eventually helped Wu achieve a sort of hegemony by replacing the traditional hegemonic Kingdom Jin. It was at this point that he came to be regarded as a genius of military strategy.

As were other philosophical and strategic texts, Sun Tzu's strategies were heavily influenced by Taoist thought, which emphasizes the interrelatedness and relativity of everything in the world. As one quotation of Taoist thought goes:

The Tao gives birth to the one.
One gives birth to two.
Two gives birth to three.
And three gives birth to ten thousand things.
The ten thousand things carry yin and embrace yang.
By combining these forces, harmony is created.

Tao not only deals with the truth of Oneness, but also the propensity for change of the Oneness. All things in the world originate at one source; all things are different but also interrelated, changing constantly in accordance with the laws of nature. There is no difference between goodness and evil, ease and difficulty, high and low, long and short. Contrasting motivating factors influencing human behavior, such as love and hate, arise from the same place, as two sides of the same coin. One can turn love into hate and hate into love, as they are not essentially different and depend on the circumstances. The same logic is applied to courage and fear, generosity and miserliness, and extrovert and introvert.

The famous story of Top Horse, Middle Horse, and Weak Horse in the Warring States Period (476–221 B.C.) exemplifies the advantages of the Taoist dialectic. Sun Bin was a master strategist who served General Tian of the Kingdom Qi. General Tian raced horses with the princes of Qi as a hobby, often wagering large sums of money. One day, General Tian came up to Sun for advice on an upcoming horse race, which seemed to be at a draw. As the usual practice went, the contest consisted of three races. The traditional strategy for victory was to pit one's best, middle, and worst horse against the similar horses of his rival. Sun Bin advised General Tian to race his worst horse against his rival's best horse, to pit his best horse against his rival's middle horse, and finally to use his middle horse to compete against his rival's worst horse. General Tian followed Sun's advice; after one loss and two wins, General Tian was declared the final winner of the contest. As a good strategist, Sun Bin saw the larger picture and understood that the goal was to win the contest, not each race.

The story clearly illustrates the Taoist concept of interrelatedness and relativity, according to which there is no absolute good or bad thing in the world. One should always use one's strong points in competing against weak points in others. The story of the Liangxiang computer company shows how ancient strategic thinking has influenced the Chinese in commercial dealings. On the whole, the Liangxiang company's computers are no match for Japanese, American, or even Taiwanese computers. But the company has adopted a strategy of selling its medium-range computer in the bottom-of-the-range international market, because the costs of the medium-range model are still low enough to allow the company to remain competitive in the bottom-of-the-range market.

Certain comparisons can be made between enterprise competitions and military warfare:

- Enterprises and armies strive for a favorable position by defeating their competitors while defending themselves.
- Competitions and wars are confrontational activities.
- Organizations must be well-organized and well-managed.
- Organizations and wars require strategies and tactics.
- The leaderships of an army and an enterprise have an important influence on the shaping of success.
- They both need high quality and committed people.
- They both thrive on information.

There does exist a fundamental difference between business and war. The former is an act of construction; the latter an act of destruction. As such, the two are diametrical.

With this in mind, we should be able to expand on those aspects of business that more closely resemble war—business competition and competitiveness. Where business and war overlap, the comparison is sound, the strategies interchangeable.

THE PRINCIPLE OF STRATEGIES

According to the opening statement of Sun Tzu's work, "War is a matter of vital importance to the state; a matter of life and death, the road either to survival or to ruin. Hence, it is imperative that it be thoroughly studied." This enunciates the importance of one aspect of Sun Tzu's principle of strategies: prudence and the need for good planning. Before a decision to wage war is made, one must engage in detailed planning. This is manifested in many parts of his writings:

> With careful and detailed planning, one can win; with careless and less detailed planning, one cannot win. How much less chance of victory has one who does not plan at all! From the way planning is done beforehand, one can predict victory or defeat.

The same is true for business competition, which concerns the survival or death of the company and the fate of shareholders, employees, customers, and the community in which it operates. Therefore, careful strategic planning is very important.

Sun Tzu emphasized first and foremost the importance of avoiding bloody conflicts as much as possible. Therefore, the highest form of victory is to conquer by strategy. To win a battle by fighting is not the best strategy; to conquer the enemy without having to resort to war is the highest, most admirable form of generalship. The next best form of generalship is to conquer the enemy with an alliance— by borrowing strengths from one's allies. This is followed by the strategy of conquering the enemy by fighting on open ground, where one can attack and withdraw easily. The worst form of generalship is to conquer the enemy by besieging walled cities. This is bound to be the most costly of endeavors. As Sun Tzu said, "For this reason, to win a hundred victories in a hundred battles is not the culmination of skills. To subdue the enemy without fighting is the supreme excellence."

To achieve this goal, one has to grasp the total picture of the situation:

> Know your enemy, know yourself, and you can fight a hundred battles with no danger of defeat. When you are ignorant of the enemy but know yourself, your chances of winning and losing are equal. If you don't know both your enemy and yourself, you are bound to perish in all battles.... Know the terrain, know the weather, and your victory will be complete.

Sun Tzu further described the necessity of appraising the following seven elements:

- the moral influence of the ruler;
- the ability of the general;
- the conditions of climate and terrain;
- the implementation of laws and rules;
- the comparative strengths of troops;
- the training of officers and soldiers; and
- the use of rewards and punishments.

MORAL INFLUENCE By moral influence, Sun Tzu meant the way in which the people are able to be in good accord with their ruler, for whom they are willing to fight through all the pitfalls involved in war. If the ruler is wise, he must first acquire the moral support of his subjects, without which he will not be able to win. To achieve this, the ruler should take care of the interests of his subjects, exercising benevolent rule and treating them as his own family members.

In the context of a war, this moral influence refers to the principle of "fighting as one man" (tong-xin). By this Sun Tzu meant that generals and soldiers share the same goals and difficulties. He wrote:

> Troops directed by a skillful general are comparable to the Shuai Ran. The Shuai Ran is a snake found in Mount Heng. Strike at its head, and you will be attacked by its tail; strike at its tail, and you will be attacked by its head; strike at its middle, and you will be attacked by both its head and its tail.... The principle of military administration is to achieve a uniform level of courage.

To achieve this goal, Sun Tzu emphasized one important principle: If a general treats his soldiers as his own beloved sons, they will stand by him until death. Many Chinese generals paid attention to this advice. Qi Ji-guang, a general in the Ming Dynasty, once said, "Although soldiers are not very smart, they are most easily moved." Because the majority of soldiers were peasants, they could be easily motivated by a little care from their generals. The famous general Yue Fei of the Song Dynasty, for example, personally prepared medicine for his soldiers.

In an extremely competitive business world, managers should endeavor to formulate a common corporate goal to be shared by all employees, so that all in the company come to view themselves as members of the group crossing the river in the same boat. They would more likely consider company affairs as their own and be willing to make personal sacrifices when needed. Only in this way can a company survive fierce competition and make full use of its competitive advantage. As Sun Tzu said, "He whose ranks are united in purpose will win."

THE ABILITY OF GENERALS A good general, according to Sun Tzu, should possess five important qualities: wisdom (*zbi*), sincerity (*cheng*), benevolence (*ren*), courage (*yong*), and strictness (*yan*). By wisdom, he meant the ability to observe changing circumstances and act accordingly, and the ability to discern and judge situations. Sincerity concerns the ability to win the complete trust of subordinates. Sun Tzu's benevolence implies deep love for one's soldiers, the ability to sympathize with their problems, and a true concern for their well-being. Courage requires a general to be brave, decisive, and able to gain victory by taking advantage of opportunities without hesitation. Strictness concerns the ability to implement discipline and mete out punishments so troops dare not violate commands or rules.

Having explained the positive qualities of a general, Sun Tzu also listed five common negative qualities that a general should discard to avert disaster:

> If reckless, he can be killed; if cowardly, he can be captured; if quick-tempered, he can easily be provoked; if sensitive to honor, he can easily be insulted; if overly compassionate to the people, he can easily be harassed.

These desirable and undesirable qualities of generalship can be used to measure corporate leadership. A corporation is similar to an army organizationally. A powerful and efficient leader is indispensable to the success of a corporation. The five positive qualities of Sun Tzu's generalship are those also needed by CEOs, whereas the five negative qualities should be avoided by any CEO. A good CEO can be expected to have a combination of the following qualities:

- broad knowledge with the capability to identify business trends and opportunities;
- the ability to establish mutual trust between management and employees;
- the capability to delegate power, while knowing how to tolerate subordinates' unavoidable mistakes;
- benevolence that understands the problems of subordinates and cares about their well-being;
- moderate amounts of compassion, to avoid easy harassment from trifles;
- the boldness to make risky decisions, while not making hasty or reckless decisions;
- the ability to combine strict discipline, meting out punishment decisively and fairly.

Sun Tzu emphasizes the basic qualities and cultivations of a military leader—his generalship rather than his military and technical background. According to Sun Tzu, "It is the business of a general to be quiet and thus ensure depth in deliberation; and to be impartial and upright, and thus keep good management." These requirements contrast with commonly accepted standards on the ability of enterprise leaders in the West, which emphasize specialized and outward abilities in such areas as manufacturing, management, finance, marketing, and creativity. For many Chinese, the technical backgrounds of a candidate can always be improved through training, but the qualities of generalship are not easy to acquire. That is why the Chinese say that "it is easier to acquire a large troop with thousands of soldiers than a good general."

CLIMATE AND TERRAIN By climate, Sun Tzu meant the changing seasons, weather, temperatures, days, and hours. Although climatic conditions represent an uncontrollable aspect of military situations, a good general knows how to use these uncontrollable components advantageously. A good general would choose the right time to fight and turn bad weather to the disadvantage of his enemy. The Russian general Kuznetzov, for example, defeated Napoleon's troops with the help of a severe Russian winter. General Zhou Yu of the Chinese Three Kingdoms Period borrowed one night's east wind to burn down his rival Cao Cao's camp. In business, a CEO also has to grapple with climatic conditions, such as the "economic climate" and the "business climate." Among these conditions are:

- Political situations, such as stability, ethnic conflicts, and wars;
- Economic cycles, such as booms, recessions, and stagnation;
- The investment climate, such as government policies, regulations, incentives, the state of technology, the protection of intellectual property, and changes in market structure;
- Other related social and cultural factors, such as changes in demography and consumer attitudes.

To be competitive, a company has to capitalize on the various changes in the economic and business environment and formulate its strategies accordingly. As in military situations, a company must realize that these environmental variables are beyond its control. It can neither command the fluctuations of economic or business environments nor dramatically affect social or cultural norms. A general must know how to fight within the constraints of climatic conditions, and a CEO of a company also has to adapt strategies for environmental constraints. On the other hand, a good general or CEO knows how to choose the best time and turn these conditions into advantages. An import substitution policy, for example, may hamper market entrance but at the same time provide opportunities for investment, which can result in access to the closed market.

Terrain refers to the area for military operation. It can be classified as accessible (we and the enemy can traverse with equal case); entangling (easy to reach, but difficult to exit); temporizing (equally disadvantageous for both the enemy and us to enter); precipitous and constricted (advantageous for whichever side occupies it first); or distant. It is the highest responsibility of a general to inquire into these various terrains with the utmost care, because these conditions will determine the chances of life and death in battle.

We should note that the word "terrain" has two dimensions: the geographical features of the battlefield and the chosen ground for fighting. The geographical features of the battlefield are largely the uncontrollable variables. Once an army is engaged in a battle on specific terrain, it will have to face the consequences incurred as a result of the terrain. Although the terrain is hard to change, a good general can decide where to fight—the battleground most favorable to the army and least favorable to the enemy. Again, as with climatic conditions, one can make a choice and turn the uncontrollable into controllable.

The same logic is also applicable for the business context, where a company has to deal with such physical and infrastructural variables as the location of its business operation. The variables include:

- the supplies of industrial and raw materials, as well as abundant cheap or high-quality labor;
- infrastructural characteristics, such as transportation systems, telecommunications, and water and power supplies; and
- access to domestic and international markets.

Again, these uncontrollable variables can be made controllable, as one can choose the best location according to one's needs. If, for example, one needs to tap cheap labor, one should move operations to a developing country. The mass migration of Taiwan's sunset industries to mainland China exemplifies this.

In sum, to cope with different climate and terrain, one should understand the general picture. As Sun said, "If one knows the place and time of the coming battle, his troops can march a thousand li and fight on the field." Although climate and terrain are for the most part unalterable, one can make a wise choice.

To cope with ever-changing situations, one should maintain a high degree of mobility and flexibility. This is the principle of "coping with change by adapting quickly." For example, the tastes and priorities of consumers change concurrent with economic changes. In an economic downturn, they tend to choose the most price-competitive goods, whereas in an economic boom many may shift their attention to designs and styles. Enterprises should change their competition strategies accordingly. Sun Tzu said:

> Of the five elements, none is ever predominant; of the four seasons, none lasts forever; of the days, some are long and others short; and of the moon, it sometimes waxes and sometimes wanes. Hence, there are neither fixed postures nor constant tactics in warfare. He who can modify his tactics in accordance with the enemy situation and thus succeed in winning may be said to be divine.

STRENGTHS Strength, for Sun Tzu, is a relative concept. There is no absolute superior strength nor absolute inferior strength. It all depends on how one can arrange it. According to Sun Tzu, "In war, number alone confers no advantage. If one does not advance by force recklessly, is able to concentrate his military power through a correct assessment of the enemy situation, and enjoys full support of his men, that would suffice." This is the principle of concentrating one's strength on the most needed area.

The principle can be applied to business, too. Sheer size may be an advantage for major enterprises, but it can also lead to an unnecessarily large organization and low efficiency. Medium and small enterprises, though restricted by limited resources, can compete with major enterprises if they can take full advantage of talents, maintain high efficiency as well as flexibility, and develop their unique products in a market niche.

For Sun Tzu, a small army may be small in comparison to a large one, but if it knows how to concentrate its small force for various battles, it may look large and eliminate the big armies one by one:

> When outnumbering the enemy ten to one, encircle him; when five times his strength, attack him; when double his strength, engage him; when evenly matched, be capable of dividing him; when slightly weaker than the enemy, be capable of defending oneself; when greatly inferior to the enemy, elude him. For no matter how obstinate a small force is, it will succumb to a larger and superior force.

Another way to enhance one's own strength is to resort to deception to confuse the enemy's perception of that strength:

> All warfare is based on deception. Therefore, when able to attack, we must pretend to be unable; when employing our forces, we must seem inactive; when we are near, we must make the enemy believe we are far away; when far away, we must make him believe we are near.

An enterprise should also hide its own real strength so its competitors do not know its real situation and direction of development. The enterprise can prepare stealthily and launch an attack where its competitors are unprepared and take action when it is unexpected.

A third method is to use spies. Sun Tzu expressed the following regarding spies:

> The reason that the enlightened sovereign and the wise general conquer the enemy whenever they move and their achievements surpass those of ordinary men is that they have foreknowledge. This "foreknowledge" cannot be elicited from spirits, nor from gods, nor by analogy with past events, nor by any deductive calculations. It must be obtained from the men who know the enemy situation.

To be competitive, an enterprise also needs information regarding its competitors, such as the development plan of its new products, operational plans, and financial situations. In this regard, Silicon Valley has learned its lessons; many Asian firms, having benefited from technologies through all possible channels, have become fierce competitors within the shortest possible time.

Sun Tzu also pointed to the importance of borrowing energy from the environment as a way to enlarge one's strength. For him, a skilled commander always uses the situation to the best advantage.

He who takes advantage of the situation in fighting uses his men as rolling logs or rocks. It is the nature of logs and rocks to stay stationary on the flat ground, and to roll forward on a slope. If four-cornered, they stop; if round-shaped, they roll. Thus, the energy of troops skillfully commanded is just like the momentum of round rocks quickly tumbling down from a mountain thousands of feet in height.

The same principle can be applied in a business context, where a company should be able to create a favorable external environment. A trading company, for example, can consolidate its position by securing good relations with suppliers or investing directly in suppliers.

DOCTRINE AND TRAINING This element stresses the importance of a whole set of regulations and rules, designation of ranks, allocation of responsibilities, and organizational structure. According to Sun Tzu, "If the army is confused and suspicious, the neighboring states will certainly cause trouble. As a saying goes: A confused army predicts victory for the enemy."

One important principle of Sun's organizational ideas is to delegate one's subordinates with necessary power. He explains one of the five preconditions for victory: "He whose generals are able and not interfered with by the sovereign will win." This is the principle of "not using the suspectable at all and using the trustworthy with full confidence" (Li and Ma, 1991). He advised a good balance between an authoritarian leader and unorganized decentralization, because either of the extremes is harmful to an organization. In a highly competitive environment, corporate managers should have sufficient power to be able to coordinate their strategies and tactics based on the changing environment. CEOs should have confidence in their subordinates and give them enough power to carry out their assignments.

For Sun Tzu, training is very important for ensuring organizational efficiency. If soldiers do not know how to follow signals, they cannot act accordingly. In a business context, companies with well-trained employees can be managed with great efficiency. Successful business organizations all over the world have good on-the-job training programs.

DISCIPLINE According to Sun Tzu, a good army always has stringent discipline, which it can achieve with an efficient reward-and-punishment system. Nevertheless, a good general should know how and when to mete out rewards or punishment. Soldiers must be treated with humanity but kept under control by iron discipline.

> If troops are punished before they have grown loyal, they will be disobedient. If not obedient, it is difficult to employ them. But if troops have become loyal, but discipline is not enforced, the general can't employ them either.

In addition, orders should be consistently carried out under strict supervision. Otherwise, troops will still be disobedient. Sun Tzu also advised a proper balance of reward and punishment: "Too frequent rewards indicate the running out of ideas; too frequent punishments indicate dire distress."

The combination of strictness and benevolence is the key to guaranteeing loyalty and discipline. This is evidenced by many examples in Chinese history. With tears in his eyes, Premier Kung Ming of the Three Kingdom Period beheaded his most beloved general when the general disobeyed his orders and lost a battle. In another example, after giving the order that soldiers not trample on crops, Cao Cao cut his own hair to show his determination to instill discipline when his own startled horse ran into the crop field.

A company that has an effective disciplinary system will be geared toward higher performance and a better competitive position. When employees are well aware of what they will receive, they will perform accordingly. Strict discipline is a reverse incentive. By introducing the system of "high rewards and severe punishment," the joint venture of Fujian-Hitachi TV Ltd. of China raised productivity. Top management members were not exempted. The chronic problem of late arrival and early departure was rooted out within a short period. Employees became more identified with the company.

Sun Tzu's strategic ideas can contribute to business competitiveness in the following areas. First, Sun Tzu emphasized the importance of moral influence within an organization. A successful manager should be able to mobilize subordinates to work as a team. Second, he stressed the importance of a broadly defined generalship for military leaders as opposed to merely their technical background. In many Asian businesses, a manager's general qualities are often viewed as much more important than technical qualifications. Third, according to Sun Tzu's views on relativism, there is no absolute superiority and inferiority in competition. One must know where one's competitive edge lies, and when, where, and how to engage in competition.

REFERENCES

"The Chinese Art of Management" (1991). *Economist*, October 26: 41.

Chu, C.-N. (1991). *The Asian Mind Game.* New York: Rawson Associates.

Griffith, Samuel B. (1971). *Sun Tzu: The Art of War.* New York: Oxford University Press.

Guo, J.-X. (1988). *Three Kingdoms and Management Strategies.* Nanning: Guanxi People's Press.

Li, F. and Hong, M. (1991). *Military Strategies and Enterprise Competitions.* Nanning: Guanxi People's Press.

Li, S.Z., Yang, X.J., and Tan, J.R. (1986). *Sun Tzu Art of War and Business Management.* Nanning: Guanxi People's Press.

Min, J.S. (1989). "The Competition Model of Sun Tzu Art of War," *The Ancient Management Philosophies and Chinese-Style Management.* Beijing: Economic and Management Press: 11–26.

Sun, H. (1991). *The Wiles of War. 36 Military Strategies from Ancient China.* Beijing: Foreign Languages Press.

Wee, C.H. (1991). *Sun Tzu: War and Management.* New York: Addison-Wesley Publishing Co.

Wu, J.L. (ed.) (1990). *Sun Tzu Art of War.* Beijing: Military Science Press.

STRATEGIC MANAGEMENT THOUGHT IN EAST ASIA

ROSALIE L. TUNG

Former U.S. Ambassador to Japan Michael Mansfield, a long-time observer of the Far East, once predicted that "it is in the Pacific and East Asia where we will see things happening in the next century, because the next century will be the 'Century of the Pacific.'" Many business and government leaders around the world have shared Mansfield's view. And there is evidence to support it. For the past several decades, many countries in East and Southeast Asia (including Japan, Taiwan, Singapore, and the Republic of Korea), as well as the territory of Hong Kong, have experienced the fastest economic growth rate in the world. More recently, the rate of industrial growth in South China has reached 40 percent annually. According to the November 28, 1992, issue of *The Economist*, if China's growth rate of the past fourteen years continues, in two decades that country will have the world's largest economy.

East and Southeast Asia also have recorded high returns on investments. The 1989 average annual returns for U.S. investments, for instance, were 31.2 percent from Singapore, 23.6 percent from Hong Kong, and 22.2 percent from Taiwan, reported *Fortune* (1991).

This regional economic transformation has changed the calculus of global competition. To compete effectively, firms must maintain a presence in East Asia. And, more importantly, they must know *how* to conduct business there. Thus, they must understand the mind-set behind East Asian business dealings.

This mind-set influences the East Asians' overall approaches toward business, including the way they define competition and cooperation. Consequently, it affects the way they formulate and execute business strategies. But the published literature provides only a little insight into the general East Asian view of the marketplace and business transaction. Writers mostly concentrate on Japanese management and decision making, and on the way these promote efficiency in industrial organizations.

There are, however, several ancient works from which East Asians generally draw their business philosophies. These books are widely disseminated and read in East Asia, but get little or no attention in the United States. They include the better-known *The Art of War* and *The Book of Five Rings*, as well as *The Three Kingdoms* and *The Thirty-Six Stratagems*.

This article provides synopses of these works and analyzes their most significant themes. Most importantly, it discusses their influence on the East Asian's approach to business cooperation and competition, and to the formulation, reformulation, and implementation of business strategies.

Reprinted from Rosalie Tung, "Strategic Management Thought in East Asia," *Organizational Dynamics*, Spring, 1994: 55–65, with permission from Elsevier Science.

THE ART OF WAR

The Art of War, or *Bingfa*, purportedly was written by Sun Tzu (spelled Sun Zi under the *pinyin* version currently used in China), a Chinese military strategist who lived about 2,500 years ago. In his foreword to *Sun Tzu: The Art of War* (1983), Noble House author James Clavell wrote, "If I were a commander-in-chief or president or prime minister, I would have written into law that all officers, particularly all generals, take a yearly oral and written examination on *The Art of War*." It was reported that Napoleon used the principles to conquer Europe, and that his violation of some of them, such as inattention to temporal conditions, led to his defeat in Russia. Admiral Togo of Japan, who defeated the Russians during the Russo-Japanese war of 1904, was a fervent student of *Bingfa*. While Sun Tzu wrote *The Art of War* for a military audience, his work is considered a "bible" or handbook for business people in East Asia. (There is a Chinese saying that "the marketplace is a battlefield.")

In the book, Sun Tzu identified six major components to success in military warfare: (1) *Moral cause*. The leader must present the morality or righteousness of going to battle. Otherwise, his troops will not be motivated to perform their best. (2) *Leadership*. The commander must be wise and courageous, but also strict and benevolent. Otherwise, his troops will disobey him, or lack full dedication to him. (3) *Temporal conditions*. When laying out plans for battle and attack strategies, the commander must be fully aware of such conditions as the seasons, weather, wind, and tide. Unexpected weather changes can thwart even the best-conceived plans. (4) *Terrain*. The commander must be completely familiar with the battle site terrain and its surrounding areas. Otherwise, his troops could fall prey to surprise attacks. (5) *Organization and discipline*. To gain the upper hand in a military confrontation and prevent chaos, troops must be extremely organized and disciplined. (6) *Espionage*. Sun Tzu discussed at length the types of spies that exist (native, inside, expendable, and surviving spies, plus double agents), as well as the circumstances under which they should be used. Without spies, it is impossible to obtain adequate information and insight about an adversary. "Know yourself, know your opponent; one hundred battles, one hundred victories," wrote Sun Tzu. "Know the weather and know the terrain, and our victory is complete."

THE BOOK OF THE FIVE RINGS

Miyamoto Musashi, a samurai in the late sixteenth and early seventeenth century, purportedly wrote *The Book of Five Rings*. When it was published in English by Bantam Books in 1982, it bore the subtitle *The Real Art of Japanese Management* and was quickly dubbed as Japan's response to Harvard's MBA.

In his later life, Musashi devotedly studied Zen philosophy and sought to unravel the connection between swordsmanship and Zen. Zen is not a religion in the Judeo-Christian tradition; rather it is a way of life, "a philosophy of willpower—one forges an iron will and an indomitable spirit." In the book, Musashi contemplates his path to enlightenment (or *heiho*). Success, he discovered, requires the following:

1. Grasping relationships and multiple perspectives. Zen believes that "the senses cannot grasp reality from one viewpoint." To gain new knowledge or find innovative solutions, the student must avoid unilateral thinking and the limitations of a one-track mind.

2. Seeking knowledge and information. Victory may be achieved when "the rhythm of each opponent" is known. This echoes Sun Tzu's famous maxim, "Know yourself, know your opponent; one hundred battles, one hundred victories."

3. Being patient. It is best to wait for the opponent to make the first move, according to *Bushido* (the way of military men).

4. Training and disciplining oneself. Through constant practice and experience, a person can excel at work (physical superiority). In addition, one has to "discipline one's spirit sufficiently" (psychological superiority). If physically and psychologically superior, "how can one lose?"

5. Disguising emotions and intentions. "(A)lways be the same way in any situation, and keep your mind in the Middle Way attitude," wrote Musashi. This echoes Confucius' preaching of moderation (*jung yung*) in all things. Furthermore, people should never reveal their *honne* (real intentions) and always "act in such a way as to not reveal the depths of your spirit to others," Musashi stated. This parallels Sun Tzu's advice: "Keep plans as dark and impenetrable as night."

6. Possessing flexibility. Despite Musashi's advocacy of the middle-of-the-road approach, he emphasizes physical, psychological, and emotional flexibility during a confrontation.

7. Using diversion. Wrote Musashi: "Once you have distracted [your opponent], gain the advantage by following with your attack." While promoting patience, Musashi also advocates swift action at the opportune moment. "It is important to chase the opponent so as not to lose the moment afforded by seizing the rhythm of the opponent's collapse," he stated. "If you lose the moment afforded by the opponent's collapse, the opponent may recover." Sun Tzu gave similar advice: to "move like a thunderbolt ... when the time is right, act swiftly and decisively."

8. Divide and conquer. "(W)hen you have seen that the ranks of the opponents have been disarrayed ... push in and strike strongly without allowing any time to lapse." Emperor Qin Shi Huang (259–210 B.C.) employed this strategy when he conquered six neighboring states to unify China. He succeeded by sowing discord among the neighboring states and then conquering them, one by one.

9. Assessing the terrain. Musashi's analysis is analogous to Sun Tzu's statement that "it is of utmost importance to force the opponent into a disadvantageous position."

THE THREE KINGDOMS

A popular Chinese classic, *The Three Kingdoms* (or *Romance of the Three Kingdoms*), was written by the fourteenth century Chinese novelist, Lo Kuan-chung. This 120-chapter book is a semi-fictional account of the struggle for control of China after the Han dynasty (China's longest-running and mightiest) collapsed in A.D. 220. The novel details the intrigues, strategies, ploys, and alliances of the three fiefdoms' leaders, and of their advisers. It includes the military strategies devised by Zhuge Liang, one of China's foremost strategists, and an incisive analysis of human nature—the good, the bad, and the ugly. It also emphasizes that kinship (a major tenet of Confucianism) is important for guiding action. This book is considered essential reading for anyone who wants to succeed in East Asia's highly competitive marketplace.

In *Sanyo's Road to Success*, Kaoru Iue, former president of Sanyo Electric Corporation of Japan, noted that his company gives each executive a lined notepad and a copy of *The Three Kingdoms* when the executive is promoted to senior management. The executives are encouraged to practice legible writing and neat arabic numerals in the notepad, so they can avoid making the costly mistakes that arise from illegible handwriting. The executives are also advised to read the book, to understand which offensive and defensive strategies apply in various situations. In short, *The Three Kingdoms* is considered an important source for survival and success tactics in a corporate jungle, and in an intensely competitive, global market.

THE THIRTY-SIX STRATAGEMS

The Thirty-Six Stratagems is based on the principles in *The Book of Changes* (or *I Ching*, which contains the basic tenets of Taoism) and on the military strategies presented in twenty-four volumes of Chinese history and literary classics (including *The Three Kingdoms*). Each stratagem, which can be represented by three or four *kanji* characters, has widespread applicability in military and nonmilitary settings—including business and interpersonal relationships. Furthermore, each stratagem can be used separately, or with several others, to create an almost infinite array of stratagems. Consequently, while all parties to a confrontation may know the thirty-six stratagems, the winner is the one who mixes and blends them into the most effective and creative strategy. This is illustrated in *Lure the Tiger out of the Mountains* (1991). Author Gao Yuan selected and translated the most popular stratagems into English and explained how they can be used under offensive, defensive, and desperate conditions. They also can be used to gain ground, to maintain an advantage, and in confused situations, noted Gao Yuan. For instance, "Lure the tiger out of the mountain," the book's title, is a stratagem. When fighting a tiger, goes the reasoning, it is foolish to wage the battle within the natural haunts of the animal—mountains and wilderness. It is better to entice the tiger into the unfamiliar, such as an interstate highway. There, the tiger is completely lost.

PRINCIPLES GUIDING THE EAST ASIAN APPROACH TO BUSINESS

As stated earlier, the purpose of this article is to analyze the important themes that underlie these works, to explain their influence on East Asian business practices, and to discuss the implications for Westerners. A comprehensive analysis reveals that these classics share twelve themes or principles, as follows:

- The importance of strategies.
- Transforming an adversary's strength into weakness.
- Engaging in deception to gain a strategic advantage.
- Understanding contradictions and using them to gain an advantage.
- Compromising.
- Striving for total victory.
- Taking advantage of an adversary's or competitor's misfortune.
- Flexibility.
- Gathering intelligence and information.
- Grasping the interdependent relationship of situations.
- Patience.
- Avoiding strong emotions.

Let's take a closer look at each of these principles.

THE IMPORTANCE OF STRATEGIES To Sun Tzu, the highest form of victory is obtained through strategy. He noted that a military commander's flaw can be "bravery without strategy." He further wrote: "To win one hundred victories in one hundred battles is not the acme of skill. To subdue the enemy without fighting [i.e., to use strategy] is the supreme excellence." Waging protracted warfare against adversaries, even if it is victorious, is costly and inefficient. But a brilliantly conceived strategy that accomplishes the same objective is swift and efficient.

From the East Asian perspective, there are preferred methods for any type of confrontation, business or otherwise. These methods can be arranged in descending order, from most to least desired.

- A brilliant strategy, to deal a swift and fatal blow to one's adversary/competitor.
- Diplomacy, to resolve a confrontation. This includes negotiations, mutual discussions, and the use of intermediaries.
- Nondiplomatic means to resolve a confrontation (open warfare). A business related example would be expensive and protracted litigation.
- Attack on a fortified city (waging warfare against a well-established opponent). This is the riskiest and costliest method.

Several stratagems emphasize strategy over physical force. For instance, "Catch the ringleader to nab the bandits" means that the use of a lot of resources to fight the enemy is a waste. It is better to capture or lure away the leader, leaving the opponent helpless. A corporate example would be a firm that hires its competitor's senior executive.

Because of the emphasis on strategy, East Asians tend to play mind games — they ferret out the hidden message in any type of communication (written, verbal, or silent) and develop a strategy to counteract the perceived message. These mind games may have contributed to the stereotyping of East Asians as "inscrutable Orientals," or as conniving Dr. Fu Manchus. During talks about normalizing diplomatic relations with China, then Secretary of State Henry Kissinger told then Chinese premier, Zhou Enlai, that he knew Zhou's strategies. "You are very smart," Zhou said. "You mean smart for an American," Kissinger retorted.

In the West, "game playing" usually has a negative connotation. In China and East Asia, however, it is considered an asset. Thus, mind games are considered manifestations of intellect. Consequently, Westerners who want to conduct business with East Asians should try to decipher the hidden messages in their East Asian partners' actions, then find ways to counter the strategies.

TRANSFORMING AN ADVERSARY'S STRENGTH INTO WEAKNESS Sun Tzu's *Bingfa* called for exhausting the opponent with false alarms, to drain the enemy before the start of the real battle. This is the stratagem of "Relax while the enemy exhausts himself." Another stratagem, "Chain together the enemy's warships," addresses the same theme. In *The Three Kingdoms*, two opposing armies prepared for a battle at sea. The troops from the fiefdom in the north were stronger, but they were vulnerable to motion sickness. The strategist in the northern kingdom advised that the troops chain their warships together, thus creating strength (i.e., stability) in the face of an impending storm. Their opponents took advantage of the reduced mobility of the ships, as well as of changes in the wind's direction (temporal conditions), by setting the warships on fire. The warships, being chained, were difficult to disengage. Thus, while the chains provided extra protection against the tide and wind, they became a liability.

Another stratagem, "Fling open the gates to the empty city," illustrates the converse principle: turning your weakness into a strength. As recounted in *The Three Kingdoms*, the great military strategist Zhuge Liang had miscalculated his opponent's plans and therefore dispatched his troops to another part of the country to await the enemy. To counter this impending attack, Zhuge Liang devised a brilliant plan. He ordered his soldiers to open the four gates to the city in which he camped. Then, he assigned twenty soldiers in civilian clothing to sweep the streets at each gate. Meanwhile, Zhuge Liang put on civilian clothes, sat on top of the city wall, and played the lute. When the leader of the advancing army heard about these activities, he was taken aback. He concluded that the peaceful scene was a facade for a terrible trap, and ordered his troops to retreat immediately. This principle is clearly illustrated in Japan's industrial development following World War II. Devastated by the war, Japan rebuilt its economy by purchasing Western technology, thus leapfrogging technological development. The disadvantage of "starting with virtually nothing" enabled Japan to establish a modern industrial base from which it could compete with the United States.

The moral of this principle is that people should not be complacent about their strengths nor abject over their liabilities—fortunes or misfortunes can reverse. According to East Asian philosophy, all events occur in cyclical patterns. (The West tends to perceive events in discrete phases.) Today's fortune might signal the beginning of a decline, and tomorrow's misfortune might mark the beginning of an upswing. Thus, it is important to avoid squandering a fortune. Instead, it should be saved for leaner times.

These themes of non-complacency, reversals of fortune, saving over spending, and accepting contradictions pervade East Asian business approaches. And they are echoed in the principles discussed below.

DECEPTION AS A MEANS TO A STRATEGIC ADVANTAGE Like "the empty city," many of the stratagems involve deceptive tactics or devices, such as creating an illusion that an attack will be launched from the east, when the real offensive will start in the west. Another tactic is to pretend to be more than one really is, or to have more than one actually has. Thus, the stratagem, "Deck the tree with bogus blossoms." This explains why designer labels and other forms of status symbols are so important in East Asia.

Because of the Judeo-Christian influence, Westerners consider such deception immoral. On the other hand, East Asians, who have no indigenous religion akin to Judaism and Christianity, consider deception a neutral term—it is amoral and acceptable if it results in a greater good. From the East Asian perspective, "the greater good" embraces the well being of the nation-state, the clan (the geographic region from which a person's ancestors came), the extended family, the nuclear family, the corporation (employer), and the self. Their order of importance, however, varies among East Asian countries. In Japan, for example, the nation-state usually tops the hierarchy. This explains the willingness of World War II *kamikaze* pilots to sacrifice their lives for the perceived good of their country. In China, Hong Kong, and Taiwan, the family is usually considered paramount. And a hierarchy exists within the family. For example, filial piety to parents is considered most important. Next comes obligations to blood brothers and "sworn" brothers, who are not related by birth but take a solemn oath of brotherhood for life. In *The Three Kingdoms*, for example, one fiefdom's leader willingly sacrifices his ambition to become king of China when he avenges the death of a sworn-brother. Said the leader to another sworn-brother:

> A brother is a limb. Wives and children are but clothes, which torn can be mended. But who can restore a broken limb? We linked our destinies ... when we vowed to die as one. My land, my family, I can spare, but not you.

Three other stratagems are significant for Westerners who want to conduct business in East Asia. They are "Pretend to be a pig in order to eat the tiger," "Play dumb while remaining smart," and "Inflict injury on oneself to win the enemy's trust." These stratagems call for the aggressor to play a fool, including such tactics as self-inflicted injury, to make the opponent complacent. Then, with the opponent's guard down, the aggressor attacks—and wins. Sun Tzu cautioned that "complacency is perhaps the greatest danger that could hasten the ruin of a successful operation." The Japanese have applied these stratagems to the automobile industry. Their generally short physiques and soft-spoken voices work to their advantage, since Americans tend to underestimate them.

The East Asian view of deception has at least one other important implication. It underscores the importance of looking beyond one's own cultural standards. What is moral or immoral in one country may not be considered such in another. This points to the need to avoid using one's own mind-set when trying to predict how members of another culture will act, and when assessing the morality of such actions.

UNDERSTANDING CONTRADICTIONS Taoism, a major school of thought in China, embraces the yin/yang principle: On the one hand, all matters have inherent contradictions and opposites; on the other hand, the opposites are unified. Lao Tzu, generally viewed as the spiritual leader of Taoism, stated that "there is one universal principle and the one becomes the many."

The national flag of the Republic of Korea bears the yin/yang symbol. Yin represents the passive, negative, dark, and female elements; yang represents the active, positive, bright, and male elements. While passivity usually is considered a negative in the West, this is not the case in East Asia. While yin and yang are opposites, they are essential for life to exist.

Since all matters have positive and negative attributes associated with them, the key to success is to accentuate the positive and minimize the negative. A person who understands these principles can use them to gain an advantage. Consider, for instance, the difference between an oak tree and a blade of grass. The tree is strong and mighty. No one can trample on it when it stands. A blade of grass, on the other hand, is small and fragile. It can be stomped on and crushed. But this picture changes during a storm: The tree may collapse under the wind's force, while the blade of grass yields to the gusts and stands firm.

Under the principles of contradictions and duality, each stratagem can be reversed, depending on the conditions. Those who transform an adversary's strength into weakness, for example, also can transform their own weaknesses into strengths. Similarly, there are two ways to apply the stratagem, "To beat the grass to startle the snake." If the objective is to scare away the snake, and not capture it, then it is acceptable to rattle the grass. But, if the objective is to capture the snake, then to create a stir would be the wrong course. The frightened snake may slither away.

COMPROMISE According to East Asian philosophy, compromise is often necessary to achieving a goal. Confucius preached moderation in all undertakings, and Musashi advocated a "middle-of-the-road" attitude. At least three of the thirty-six stratagems call for compromise: (1) "Trade a brick for a piece of jade." (2)

"Sacrifice the plum tree for the peach tree." (3) "Snag the enemy by letting him off the hook." These stratagems involve baiting an opponent with a small gain, to get an even bigger prize. Consequently, gift-giving, lavish entertainment, and bribery are common practices in East Asian societies. Indeed, research has shown a strong correlation between high-context cultures, characterized by implicit communication and extensive networks, and the use of questionable payments. An estimated 70 percent of the world's population belong to high-context cultures, including East Asians, Arabs, and Mediterraneans. Low-context societies include the United States and most of northern Europe.

There are other ramifications. Compromise requires an ongoing relationship (whether cooperative or competitive); otherwise, the parties have nothing to trade off. This accounts, at least in part, for the East Asian's emphasis on developing ongoing relationships. Also, many U.S. respondents view their Korean counterparts as illogical or inconsistent. Some do not understand the Korean penchant to concede major issues yet remain adamant about trivial matters, according to a study of business negotiations between Americans and Koreans. This may be explained either by the compromise principle or by the difference between what the Americans and the Koreans consider to be major and minor issues. Different cultures place different values on different outcomes.

STRIVING FOR TOTAL VICTORY While East Asian philosophy emphasizes compromise, it also stresses the need to strive for total victory. In other words, a temporary victory should not lull people to complacency—a false sense of security. Then, they will lose sight of the ultimate objective. The stratagems that address this principle are "Shut the door to catch the thief" and "Pull the ladder after the ascent." In other words, cut off escape routes so opponents or competitors cannot rebuild their strength.

This principle has important implications. People should not be complacent or careless during good times. And they should think about the long-term consequences of their actions. They must project their opponent's next move, to intercept that move.

TAKING ADVANTAGE OF AN ADVERSARY'S OR COMPETITOR'S MISFORTUNE Since East Asians believe that fortunes and misfortunes occur in cyclical patterns, they try to make the most of current situations. Consequently, if an adversary/competitor is down, they seize that opportunity to eliminate the adversary. As Musashi wrote, "It is of utmost importance to force the opponent into a disadvantageous position" and seize "the rhythm of the opponent's collapse." The related stratagems are "Loot a burning house" and "Take the opportunity to pilfer a goat," as well as "Watch fires burning across the river" and "Fish in troubled water."

From the Western perspective, these teachings are immoral and unethical. But East Asians are a pragmatic people. The Chinese emphasize pragmatism even more than their counterparts in Japan and Korea. This partly explains why religion and politics do not play significant roles in the daily life of the average person from the People's Republic of China, or of those from Hong Kong or Taiwan. Although China is communistic, a surprisingly small percentage of its population belongs to the Communist Party. In Hong Kong, the majority of residents are ethnic Chinese. But most don't mind British rule as long as Hong Kong provides a favorable economic environment for entrepreneurs.

The Chinese emphasis on pragmatism led to the development of the last—and what many consider the most important—of the thirty-six stratagems: "Run away." Under extreme conditions (when faced with imminent defeat), it is better to escape than to commit suicide or get killed. Since the Chinese believe that fortunes and misfortunes occur in a cyclical fashion, they believe escape leaves them a chance to regain their strength and position. As Sun Tzu noted, "When facing death, the struggle for survival will give new birth." Death eliminates such a possibility.

The Japanese are taught that facing death is courageous. The Chinese, on the other hand, agree with Sun Tzu that "Bravery without strategy is folly." Han dynasty founder Liu Bang was defeated several times before he conquered his opponents and became emperor. He had known when to retreat and regroup his troops. In contrast, his arch rival Xiang Yu, who won many battles, committed suicide after his first defeat.

Some people attribute this difference between the Japanese and Chinese to the size (land mass) of their respective countries and to the supply of natural resources in each. Japan's limited land mass and few natural resources led its people to believe that death is preferred, since there is no escape. (In fact, death and stoicism are major tenets of Zen philosophy.) On the other hand, the Chinese, who believe it is always possible to escape and regain strength, have an extensive land mass and vast natural resources.

FLEXIBILITY Nature inspired East Asian philosophy, and thus appears in many related analogies. Sun Tzu, for instance, invoked nature when he preached the importance of flexibility—adapting to changing conditions and fortunes.

> Know when to fight and when not to fight ... (T)he laws of military operations are like water ... Consequently, just as water ceaselessly changes its flow, there are no constant methods of directing military operations. The one who is able to alter and revise his tactics and strategy according to the enemy's situation will be considered as divine as a god.

According to Sun Tzu, when military capability is ten times that of the opponent, force the enemy to surrender. When military capability is five times that of the opponent, it is advisable to attack. When military capability is only two times that of the adversary, divide the enemy's troops. When both sides have the same military capability, use strategy and deception. When military capability is less than the enemy's, avoid confrontation and flee. Thus the stratagem "Run away," discussed in the last section. Another stratagem says, "Attack when near, befriend when distant." Since a military campaign that takes place far away might exhaust the troops, it is best to substitute diplomacy.

This emphasis on flexibility accounts, in part, for the East Asian perspective of written legal contracts as organic documents that can be altered as circumstances change. In the West, a signed contract is considered sacrosanct, with inviolate terms. This difference will continue to frustrate many Westerners who want to conduct business in East Asia.

GATHERING INTELLIGENCE AND INFORMATION As noted earlier, both Sun Tzu and Miyamoto Musashi strongly emphasized the importance of gathering information and intelligence about the opponent or competitor. Such information can be obtained from a variety of sources, such as spies. Industrial espionage, in fact, has become a common practice. Other ways to gather information include entering into alliances with local partners and employing local nationals. Businesses have increasingly realized that global competition demands more and more collaboration with companies from around the world—competition and cooperation become opposite sides of the same coin.

Gathering intelligence also means spreading erroneous information to contaminate and frustrate the opponents' strategies. ("Let the enemy's own spy sow discord in the enemy camp.") So-called expendable spies intentionally provide wrong information to the opponent. They usually are disposed of or executed, once the opponent discovers the deception.

In addition to technical information, knowledge includes intelligence about key players. It takes a long time to accurately assess human nature, however. So East Asians focus a lot of energy on developing relationships and finding out the true intentions of business counterparts. This explains, in part, the slow pace of East Asian business, compared with the West.

GRASPING THE INTERDEPENDENT RELATIONSHIP OF SITUATIONS The inherent duality and contradictions (yin/yang) in all matters may not always be obvious. But they must be unearthed to be used effectively. Miyamoto Musashi, a disciple of Zen philosophy, stressed the need to do this from different perspectives.

A good illustration of this principle is the Japanese saying, "When the wind blows, it is good for the makers of wooden tubs." According to a Japanese professor, the logic behind this is as follows: In inclement weather, people become sad. To overcome their depression, they play a stringed instrument called the *shamisen*. Cats are killed to make the *shamisen* (its strings are made from catgut) and, if the cat population gets depleted, there is a corresponding proliferation of mice. Without cats, the mice embolden and then gnaw at the wooden tubs that are used to store grain. When holes develop in the tubs, the tubs must be replaced. That creates an increased demand for wooden tubs. This is good for the makers of wooden tubs.

Hall and Hall (1987) noted that this logic seems convoluted, but "it expresses quite accurately the Japanese preoccupation with being able to see the long-term implications of actions as well as the relationships between apparently unrelated systems." A Western businessperson has to understand this East Asian preoccupation with long-term implications, and with finding connections between seemingly unrelated matters. Awareness of the attempts to link matters can help Westerners detect East Asian mind games.

PATIENCE Experienced Westerners who have succeeded in East Asia readily admit that patience was a major requisite to their success. Certainly, the importance of patience differs across countries. Koreans, for instance, generally make quicker decisions than their Chinese and Japanese counterparts. But, overall, East Asian business requires patience, because it takes time to develop relationships.

There are several reasons why the East Asian pace is slower. One is the focus on the long-term implications of actions. A second reason is the importance attached to developing and nurturing human relationships. (An accurate assessment of human nature can only be made after an extended period of time, as noted above.) A third reason is the belief that everything occurs cyclically. If East Asians lose their fortunes, and the moment is inopportune, they will wait patiently until the situation reverses.

Patience was stressed in *Bushido*, which cautions against launching a first strike. Consider the way that sumo wrestlers sit on their haunches, to wear down their opponents. Unlike a boxing match, which is filled with action (punches and counter-punches), inaction is a significant part of a sumo wrestling match. Chinese history is filled with people who waited for as long as thirty years to avenge a wrong.

AVOIDING STRONG EMOTIONS As noted earlier, Confucius cautioned against taking extreme positions. Sun Tzu warned that a military commander should never fly into a rage. These admonishments are the roots of the East Asian aversion to harboring or displaying strong emotions, since they may ruin carefully conceived plans. In fact, statistics show that an overwhelming majority of North American murders can be traced to misplaced passions. On the other hand, while East Asians recognize that strong emotions can confuse or distort logical thinking and action, they also use emotions to conquer opponents and competitors. Thus the stratagem, "Provoke strong emotions."

Another stratagem is "Use a woman to ensnare a man." This explains why the Japanese and Koreans often use women and other sensual entertainments to improve their chances of making desirable business transactions.

Again, there are differences across countries. In comparison with the Japanese and Chinese, the Koreans are emotional. In Japan, for example, it is considered bad form for a widow to cry incessantly during her husband's funeral; in Korea, it is bad form if a person does not cry loudly, even at a distant cousin's funeral. Common occurrences in Korean business offices include chest-beating, desk-pounding, and shouting matches.

CONCLUSION AND DISCUSSION

This article has identified twelve themes underlying East Asia's approach to competing and cooperating, as well as formulating and implementing strategies. These themes may appear in a variety of forms. As Lao Tzu said, "There is one universal principle, and the one becomes the many." In Sun Tzu's discourse on potentials, he noted that Chinese music only has five notes. But the notes can be combined, to produce an infinite array of melodies. Similarly, the five basic color pigments can be mixed and blended into a vast and diverse range of hues. So, the twelve themes may be used in isolation, reversed, or combined to produce more stratagems.

While some of the themes and stratagems may contradict Western principles, it would be inappropriate to judge East Asians with Western morality standards. It is true that "culture" may sometimes be used as a ploy to gain a negotiating advantage. For example, an East Asian partner might try to get a concession by using the phrase "this is how things are done in the East," even if the phrase is untrue. Westerners must be aware of the East Asian mind-set, outlined in this article, to distinguish between a cunning strategy and a genuine cultural difference.

The article stresses common themes. But it is equally important to recognize the significant differences between East Asian cultures. As Lao Tzu said, "The one becomes the many." While people from Japan, Korea, China, Hong Kong, and Taiwan may derive their business sense from the same philosophers, they sometimes differ significantly in the way they interpret and apply the philosophies. Thus, the Chinese prefer escape; the Japanese often choose death. The Japanese avoid public displays of emotion; the Koreans condone it.

These differences are further compounded by foreign religious influences. For example, there are many Chinese and Japanese Buddhists, as well as Korean Christians. Similarly, overseas travel and study, as well as social and business contact with foreigners, helped reshape the East Asian mentality and mind-set. Consequently, while it is wrong to assume that East Asians are exactly like Westerners, it is equally wrong to stereotype them as homogeneous. Again, recall Sun Tzu's favorite maxim, "Know yourself, know your opponent; one hundred battles, one hundred victories." To succeed at global competition, we must try to understand ourselves and our overseas counterparts—not just certain management practices and procedures, but also their motivations, morality, and philosophies on cooperating and competing. Such knowledge may increase significantly the Westerner's chances of sharing some of the economic fruits of a transformed East Asia.

QUESTIONS: SECTION TWO

SUN TZU'S STRATEGIC THINKING AND CONTEMPORARY BUSINESS
MIN CHEN

1. Chen lists several analogies between business competition and warfare in general. Do you agree these commonalities hold true? Are there others?

2. Do you agree that military action is destructive while business competition is constructive?

3. Chen discusses the tenets of Sun Tzu's *Art of War*: the need for planning, the forms of generalship, and the seven elements. What might a Western strategist learn from Sun Tzu's approach?

4. Chen mentions the strong relationship between family ties and success or failure in business in Asia. Does this relationship also hold true in the U.S.? How might this relationship affect business strategy?

STRATEGIC MANAGEMENT THOUGHT IN EAST ASIA
ROSALIE L. TUNG

1. What might a Western leader learn from each of the twelve themes Tung draws from Asian literature?

2. Although these themes help in understanding thinking in East Asian countries, Tung warns there are limitations to applying them. What are these limitations, and what are the implications to understanding strategy?

3. Tung draws from the several seminal sources of influence on East Asian business strategy. Are there fundamental sources of influence on American business strategy? If so, what are these sources, and what influence do they have?

3

ANCIENT FOOTPRINTS

Gates may have the mind of Machiavelli and the soul of a satrap, but when it comes to being a worthy assassino, he's a day late and a dagger short.

—Owen Edwards (2001), describing Microsoft's Bill Gates

Section Three traces the steps of a political theorist from the 16th century, as well as several ancient philosophers from Greece and China. Like the articles on Pericles and Sun Tzu, the articles in this section demonstrate that corporate leaders of the future stand to learn a great deal from the past. The first selection derives archetypes for leaders of modern companies from writings of Machiavelli and Lao-tzu. "Managing Change: Views from the Ancient Past" reaches back to Greek thinkers in order to clarify modern arguments about the very possibility of strategy in rapidly changing conditions. In this selection, metaphor lends insight into the way strategists can organize ambiguity and manage change.

Business practitioners and scholars have questioned whether prevailing leadership styles are consistent with the modern realities of flattened organizational hierarchies and increasingly highly skilled workers. What sort of leader is best able to create conditions in which innovation flourishes? In the first selection, "Would You Want Machiavelli as Your CEO?," two poles of a continuum of leadership style are clarified by drawing from Machiavelli's 16th-century political treatise, *The Prince,* and the Chinese *Tao Te Ching*, which was written more than two thousand years ago. These historical models allow the reader to consider the implications of autocratic and empowering leaders to the manners in which corporations are controlled, not only by management, but by shareholders, employees, and the government. It turns out that many features of the Taoist approach seem to be more appropriate in attracting highly skilled and self-motivated workers and the innovation they foster, than the Machiavellian leader's highly controlling and manipulative style. Leaders who "judge their own leadership effectiveness by their ability to inculcate it within others" are no longer an ideal in companies, but a necessity.

All metaphors have limitations, and Taoism is no exception. Not all of the Taoist characteristics—extreme piousness, avoidance of greatness, and the aversion to competition—ring true for corporate leadership. When a company's very survival is at stake, conditions may demand a more dominant leader with selected Machiavellian characteristics. The state of the organization and its competitive environment determine which attributes should be emphasized. Here we see that committing a "cardinal sin" of English composition—mixing metaphors—is fair game in business strategy. A single lens is often inadequate to capture the complex and dynamic interactions between a company and its environment.

How do leaders conceive of change, and what does this imply for managing it? The second article, "Managing Change: Views from the Ancient Past," sheds light on a very modern challenge, and suggests that the ubiquitous assumption of constant change in strategy has grave consequences. Arguments from Heraclitus and Parmenides on the existence and meaning of change demonstrate that if "everything is changing," strategic management is futile. Plato and Aristotle recognized this and, unwilling to fall victim to change, devised contrasting approaches to managing it. The message to leaders is that they acknowledge change without over-emphasizing it. Strategy assumes that some things *are* stable. The leader's job is to wade through conditions of change and ambiguity and find principles that transcend it. Plato's strategy to manage change is to identify values, unwavering ideals, a mission, and a vision that supercede the "flotsam and jetsam." The Platonic leader does so in isolation of others who lack his intellect and moral superiority. Aristotle, on the other hand, encourages the involvement of everyone in managing change, by collectively designing an organization's goals and striving to reach them.

WOULD YOU WANT MACHIAVELLI AS YOUR CEO? THE IMPLICATIONS OF AUTOCRATIC VERSUS EMPOWERING LEADERSHIP STYLES TO INNOVATION

CYNTHIA K. WAGNER

The trend towards reducing layers of management in companies appears to be fact, not fashion. Walter B. Wriston (1990), the former chairman of Citibank and Citicorp, has attributed the inevitability of flattened organizations to accelerated information flow, lessened micromanagement, and the growing importance of intellectual capital relative to physical capital. Belasco and Stayer (1994, p. 31) echo these insights:

> ... in the mid-nineteenth century, markets were local or national, communication took days or weeks, work was unskilled and manual, workers were uneducated, and stability was the rule ... Markets are now global, electronic highways enable instant communication and rapid competitive responses, work involves the creation, transmission, and manipulation of information and knowledge, and workers are highly educated.

These organizational changes are consonant with the dimensions of the innovative, idea-rich climates described by Ekvall (1993), which stress freedom, trust, playfulness, dynamism, and risk-taking behavior. Although fostering innovation is recognized as key to maintaining competitive advantage, business people and management scholars alike have raised serious questions as to whether prevailing corporate leadership models are appropriate to the new organizational reality. Autocratic styles, in particular, are under fire.

> Despite having been discussed for years, the problems of centralization, autocratic management style, and poor communication linkages between top management and the rest of the firm still plague American business. (Krachenberg, 1993)

> Now advanced technology is spread throughout the world, and we need employee commitment more than control and compliance. Nevertheless, the dominant style of U.S. managers still seems to be autocratic, and we are losing our position as the dominant economic power. (Huszezo, 1990)

Developing leadership models appropriate to the contemporary business environment also has become a major concern of the American Assembly of Collegiate Schools of Business (1993). The perceived lack of leadership prowess gained through conventional business education has led to the design of radically new programs and curricula. Clearly, the challenge of guiding companies successfully into the next century demands that the leadership lag be addressed.

Classics from both Western and Eastern literary traditions provide a highly instructive antidote to the issues surrounding contemporary corporate leadership style. Two extreme models—autocratic, centralized, or top down leadership, and the more participatory, democratic style—are vividly illustrated by, respectively, the political theorist Niccolo Machiavelli and the ancient Chinese thinker, Lao-tzu. Analysis of their approaches to leadership helps clarify the tendencies that predominate in companies now and envision the styles appropriate to less hierarchical, innovative companies. The discussion below weaves together excerpts from Machiavelli's *The Prince* (1531), Lao-tzu's *Tao Te Ching* (circa 531 B.C.) and contemporary management scholar Henry Mintzberg's article "Who Should Control the Corporation?" (1984). Machiavelli's and Lao-tzu's concepts of leadership first are contrasted. Mintzberg's framework of corporate control methods is then used as a vehicle for translating the Machiavellian and Taoist principles to the contemporary business context. Finally, Argyris and Schon's theories of organizational learning are applied in order to further support the suitability of many of the dimensions of the Taoist style for leading innovative organizations, and to provide guidance as to how companies can make the transition from autocratic to more empowering leadership styles.

MACHIAVELLI AND LAO-TZU: THE NIGHT AND DAY OF LEADERSHIP STYLES

It is not unusual to read of the actions of a leader described as "Machiavellian," normally in a pejorative sense. But what does it really mean to be associated today with the writing of a 15th century Italian aristocrat? An officer of the Florentine Republic, Machiavelli led diplomatic missions, mostly of a military nature. When the republic was overthrown in 1512, he was banished from Florence for suspected crimes against the State and began to develop a political theory that has endured to the present day. In *The Prince*, Machiavelli was concerned with one central issue: what qualities must a person have to gain and retain power? As will become evident, the pragmatic Machiavelli admonished leaders to act out of self-interest and with low regard for underlings. In contrast, Lao-tzu believed that only in serving others could one effectively lead them. The Chinese philosopher lived two thousand years before Machiavelli, from 604 B.C. to 531 B.C., and was an archivist at the Chou court. He is generally thought to have written Tao Te Ching as his philosophical treatise; however, its authorship remains somewhat of a mystery. The Tao Te Ching is considered to be the main scripture of Taoism, which along with Buddhism and Confucianism is one of the three great religions of China. The treatise has provided guidance on human conduct to millions of people over the ages.

The Machiavellian and Taoist leadership styles can be contrasted along several dimensions (Exhibit 1). Machiavelli's personal and professional philosophies are inseparable. In a nutshell, a leader must do whatever is necessary in order to gain and maintain power whenever, wherever. Power, which is an end in itself, is gained by manipulating subordinates to serve one's own purposes. The leader must find a way to be feared by others, yet not hated. Trust has no place in

| EXHIBIT 1 | SUMMARY COMPARISON/CONTRAST OF MACHIAVELLIAN AND TAOIST LEADERSHIP STYLES | |

Qualities as a Leader	Machiavellian Style	Taoist Style
Leadership Philosophy	Secure and maintain power to further self interest.	Never reach for the great and you will achieve greatness. Act for the people's benefit. To govern others, place yourself below them; to lead you must learn to follow.
Personal Philosophy	Inseparable from professional mission. Only war is important. Learn how not to be good when necessary. However, avoid being caught doing evil; escape a bad reputation despite vices.	Be yourself, believe in yourself; don't compare self with others or compete. Think of yourself as no better than others.
Attitude Towards Power	Power is an end in itself. Know how to use force; be a fox to avoid traps and a lion to frighten wolves.	Don't try to control, coerce, or dominate. Gentleness overcomes hardness.
Relationship with Subordinates	Strive to be feared, not loved; but avoid being hated. Manipulate, coerce others as necessary. Underlings will not keep promises, so neither should you.	The best leader is one who the people hardly know exists; next best is a leader who is loved; next, one who is feared; the worst is despised. He who has power over others cannot empower himself. Care for, nourish, comfort other people. Do not oppress or manipulate. Serve as an example to others; don't impose your will.
Honesty/Trust	Be evil and deceitful when necessary. Don't trust too little or too much.	Trust people, and they will be trustworthy.
Self-Control	Maintain it, always.	Mastering yourself is true power; but the more powerful you grow, the more humility you need.
Education/Training	Keep yourself and soldiers trained, disciplined. Know the terrain. Always have a remedy for unforeseen events.	Learn by looking within self, not by practicing. Learn simplicity, compassion, patience. The more you know, the less you understand.
Role Models	Imitate successful leaders who came before.	Look inside for guidance.

Machiavelli's world, where subordinates will not keep their promises and deserve nothing but the same in return. Charity is stripped of any humanitarian dimension, as being good is important only so far as it furthers a leader's power over others. In fact a person must learn evil and deceit, how *not* to be good, when necessary. The trick is not to be caught; to keep the people's support by maintaining an impression of goodness, even though it may well be a cover for wrongdoing. And if force is necessary to obtain power, so be it. The Machiavellian leader must ensure that underlings are well trained to serve his or her interests, and that they have sound knowledge of the environment. For guidance on leadership, one must look to those in the past who were successful in gaining and maintaining power and then imitate their behavior.

The Tao Te Ching's leadership philosophy is one of benevolence, individualism, and self confidence, yet lack of pretension. A leader should not gain power at the expense of others. A leader will achieve prominence not by consciously seeking it; but, in fact, by denying it. Purism and piousness will bring greatness. The *Tao Te Ching* promotes gentleness over force; softness over hardness. Control, domination, and intimidation are disdained, as they will elicit unwanted fear and hatred. Trust others, according to Lao-tzu, and they will be trustworthy. Instead of focusing on gaining power over others, true power is obtained by mastering and controlling oneself. The leader should be in the background, invisible to subordinates, as he or she nourishes others and serves as an example to them. A leader must develop a sense of individuality, and not compare himself or herself with others or compete with them. The Taoist manager looks within for guidance and strives to achieve simplicity, compassion and patience.

MACHIAVELLI AND LAO-TZU: RELEVANCE TO THE LEADERSHIP OF MODERN CORPORATIONS

How can the leadership models of 16th-century Florentine political circles and ancient China inform modern corporate management? In "Who Should Control the Corporation," Henry Mintzberg (1984) considers the role of corporations in fulfilling economic goals, as well as in ameliorating social conditions within and beyond the company. He delineates a variety of means by which corporations can be influenced by managers, employees, shareholders, and external stakeholders, such as the government and public interest groups. His portfolio of choices provides a useful vehicle for contrasting the control methods that would be aligned with Machiavelli and Lao-tzu, were they corporate leaders. What is of even more importance to the appropriateness of the two leadership styles to innovation, however, is the response they elicit from the various internal and external stakeholders. The comparison below demonstrates an inconsistency between the Machiavellian leader's goals and those of the various stakeholders. This inconsistency becomes even more striking and untenable in a context where employees are highly educated; the centralized and self serving autocratic management style elicits the very control it shuns. In comparison, the goals of the Taoist leaders and the stakeholders—particularly the modern knowledge worker—are consistent.

METHODS OF CORPORATE CONTROL IMPLIED BY EACH LEADERSHIP STYLE

Mintzberg's eight alternatives for controlling the corporation range from **nationalization**, where the government owns and operates a firm or an entire industry to further its social agenda, to **restoration** of corporate control, in which direct owners operate the company only to maximize profits. Between these two alternatives lie several that emphasize social influence: **democratization**, which is achieved by assigning employees and/or external public interest groups to decision-making bodies at the corporate level and/or below; **regulation** by governmental agencies that penalize a company for wrongdoing; and **pressure** from ad hoc public interest groups. Two other approaches emphasize the corporation's economic responsibility: that in serving economic goals, social goals will be met secondarily and thus can be **ignored**; and that in some cases companies can be **induced** with incentives to fulfill social goals, such as equal opportunity. The remaining alternative represents a happy medium between attention to economic and social goals; corporate leaders can be **trusted** to explicitly recognize the need to pursue both agendas.

Mintzberg's eight approaches to control can be further categorized on the basis of two dimensions: (one) whether or not they entail recognition of social responsibility by corporate leadership; and (two) the degree of influence on the part of governmental or nongovernmental forces exerted on corporate leadership (Exhibit 2). Four of the approaches—nationalization, democratization, inducement, and regulation—are clustered in the area of high control and high degree of social responsibility. The extreme case is nationalization, in which corporate leadership carries out the social program of the government; democratization implies

---

EXHIBIT 2   CATEGORIZATION OF MINTZBERG'S EIGHT METHODS OF CONTROLLING THE CORPORATION ON THE BASIS OF DEGREE OF SOCIAL RESPONSIBILITY RECOGNIZED BY THE LEADERSHIP AND DEGREE OF CONTROL EXERTED ON LEADERSHIP

recognition of social concerns by encouraging involvement of employees and/or other interests in decision-making. Inducement involves a less comprehensive effort on the part of the company to achieve social goals, and also is less intrusive as the company responds to voluntary incentives. Regulation represents concerted governmental influence in response to a company's lack of attention to social issues. At the other extreme, that of low social responsibility and low degree of control, are ignoring social issues and restoring control to owners. Restoration means that the corporate leadership believes their goal is to maximize shareholder profits, period, and without any interference. Leaders who ignore social goals believe that by fulfilling their economic purpose unencumbered, they will naturally remain in line with social issues. Pressure involves a limited injection of control to achieve a social goal and normally involves public interest groups. Finally, trustworthy corporate leadership represents the highest degree of social responsibility achieved with the lowest degree of control by stakeholders, as these leaders explicitly recognize their social responsibility as part of the corporation's mission, and thus do not necessitate prompting.

Which of these approaches to corporate control would be most aligned with the autocratic versus empowering styles? Recall that the Machiavellian leader is self serving, and uses the company and its employees as a means to gain and maintain his or her own power. This posture is maintained twenty-four hours a day, without exception. Whatever it takes to do this is fair game. The Machiavellian CEO manipulates others, deceives them when necessary, and coerces them into behavior that serves his or her end. Yet the leader creates an image that betrays this tyrannical behavior. Subordinates are expected to obey orders, and their training is to support the leader's position. Their loyalty, however, is not to be trusted, and they are constantly to be kept in line. The Machiavellian CEO, then, would most likely lean towards ignoring social responsibility or, if possible, restoring control to himself or herself alone. With these two methods, the leader is best able to operate without stakeholder influence or concern for social goals. The other six alternatives would not be palatable to Machiavellian leadership, as each entails at least some degree of attention to social responsibility and each involves a degree of stakeholder control that the Machiavellian leader would reject.

In contrast, the Taoist CEO is an unassuming, almost reluctant, leader whose very lack of desire for power brings it. The Taoist leader focuses on developing herself or himself and serves as an example for employees. As one quietly gives to others and provides an environment in which they can flourish, power and recognition will be gained; yet once attained the leader becomes all the more reticent. Force has no place in this company. Employees are encouraged, gently, to look within and find their own way. Referring to Exhibit 2, the Lao-tzu style would likely be aligned with explicit recognition of social concerns within and outside the company and, therefore, be trusted.

IMPLICATIONS OF LEADERSHIP STYLE TO STAKEHOLDERS The Machiavellian CEO prefers methods that entail no stakeholder control, while the Taoist CEO, who explicitly recognizes the corporation's social responsibility, renders stakeholder control unwarranted. But what sort of control methods would be elicited from the various stakeholders of the corporation if their leader were Machiavellian or Taoist?

The employees of a corporation headed by a Machiavellian leader would actively seek participation in decision-making via democratization, as well as through the *ad hoc* application of pressure by, for instance, striking. They would not accept laissez faire responses such as trusting or ignoring leaders with such a heavy handed and top down approach. This response would be amplified as the educational levels of the employees—and thus their contribution and value to the company—increased. Employees would be likely, however, to trust Taoist leadership. Democratization measures might be encouraged, but there would be little reason for external control beyond this.

The shareholders of a corporation are likely to see the corporation primarily as a vehicle for economic gain, which will be reflected in stock prices, and less so for furtherance of social goals; they therefore would prefer laissez-faire approaches to corporate control. But when a Machiavellian leader is at the helm of an organization, shareholder objectives would very well not be served by those of self-interested management. Therefore, shareholders could not trust the corporation's leadership; and it would be unwise to ignore it. They might prefer restoring control to ownership, but to themselves, not to the Machiavellian leader. If restoring control to ownership were not feasible, shareholders might resort to the less intrusive and nongovernmental external control methods, such as exerting pressure on corporate leadership to change or resign and/or demanding more representation on the Board of Directors.

Because the shareholders' primary concern is with the economic well being of the corporation, they would probably encourage Taoist leadership to ignore social issues as much as possible, and assume that in the course of fulfilling economic goals, social goals would also be realized. However, so long as the company has shown acceptable financial performance, shareholders might also be willing to trust leaders who have both social and economic goals in mind.

From the standpoint of the government, a Machiavellian approach to leading a corporation—one that completely neglects social goals in light of extreme self-interest—is likely to meet with increased control via regulation and inducement, and, at the very extreme, nationalization. The government would not accept any of the laissez-faire approaches to control in this situation. With the Taoist leader at the helm, however, the government would be much more likely to trust corporate leadership to perform both its economic and social functions and find it unnecessary to intervene.

These findings make evident the implications of leadership style to the type and degree of control exerted by internal and external forces (Exhibit 3). Autocratic leadership is self defeating; the very desire to pursue self interest above all and independently of influence is precisely what elicits stakeholder control of the organization. The autocratic approach elicits control not only from employees, but the government and also the shareholders, who are concerned that the self serving behavior of the Machiavellian CEO may not be in the best interest of

EXHIBIT 3	APPLICATION OF MINTZBERG'S PORTFOLIO OF CORPORATE CONTROL METHODS TO THE MACHIAVELLIAN AND TAOIST LEADERSHIP STYLES AND STAKEHOLDER GROUPS			
	Corporate Control Methods Aligned with Leadership Style	Employees	Shareholders	Government
Machiavellian Leader (Autocratic)	Restore control to self	Democratize decision-making	Restore control to shareholders	Regulate company
	Ignore social responsibility	Pressure top management (e.g., to strike)	Pressure top management (e.g., to resign)	Induce social responsibility
				Nationalize company
Taoist Leader (Empowering)	Trust: recognition of both economic and social responsibility	Trust leaders	Trust leaders Ignore social responsibility	Trust leaders

returns. In contrast, the control methods preferred by empowering leadership and the control methods elicited from stakeholders are more consistent. Taoist leaders want their motives to fulfill both social and economic goals to be trusted, and in fact they *would* likely be trusted by employees, the government, as well as shareholders.

THEORIES OF ORGANIZATIONAL LEARNING: MAKING THE TRANSITION FROM POWER TO EMPOWERMENT

Theories of organizational learning developed by Argyris and Schon (1978) provide further support for the suitability of the Taoist leadership style to innovative climates, and also offer insight into intervention approaches that help facilitate the transition from autocratic to more empowering leadership.

Leadership characterized by the desire to control and self interest—and an organization that experiences frequent demand from employees for increased participation in decision-making, increased control by shareholders and the government—reflect Argyris and Schon's "single loop learning" or the Organizational I (O-I) learning system. This model is one in which innovation would be stifled, as it implies an organization that is "highly competitive, rarely additive, low in openness, trust and risk taking, high in closedness, mistrust, and emphasis on not rocking the boat" (Argyris and Schon, 1978, p. 123).

The Taoist leadership style mirrors the "deutero learning system." In contrast to the single loop system, in which problems are framed and solved within the limited boundaries of the existing organization, deutero learning encourages continual development of new underlying norms in response to changing demands of the technological, economic, social, and political environment of an organization. This dynamic and highly innovation climate would be best led by a Taoist leader, who helps others reach their potential without intimidating or dominating them, and gains their trust.

Although picturing the "before" and "after" organizational states is necessary for change to occur, mapping the means to make the transition from the single loop to the deutero learning systems is, as Argyris and Schon admit, much more difficult. The leap requires that an organization gain the ability to question its fundamental objectives as well as the means by which it achieves them. This move from single loop to double loop learning then must be institutionalized, such that the process of change itself becomes embedded in the organization, and a deutero learning system is established. The first step in the transition is the recognition of the inadequacy of the prevailing system for addressing the organization's problems. This recognition is then followed by open organizational inquiry into the means by which to facilitate the change to a more effective system. The hitch is that concealment of motives is inherent within Machiavellian norms. The single loop learning system inhibits the very inquiry that sets a precedent for the transition. To make matters worse, the transition requires that top leadership commit itself to change. This is unlikely in an organization led by a CEO ingrained in autocratic principles, and whose selfish goals are best served by maintaining single loop learning.

It follows that intervention into the Machiavellian led organization must be initiated by the Board of Directors. And, if intervention fails to enlighten the autocratic CEO, and chances are it *will* fail, it is the Board's responsibility to replace the Machiavellian leader with one more supportive of the deutero learning system aligned with continual innovation. Once this leadership is in place, however, the transition process has just begun. Company leadership must then recognize the necessity of altering the learning system of the entire organization, ensuring that the new model supplants the old company-wide. Too, the employees must be open, or opened, to disseminating the learning system throughout the organization. Otherwise the directive simply represents a top down maneuver that reinforces the traditional Model O-I autocratic mode. Almost two decades before the recent popularity of "re-engineering" organizations, which emphasizes the increased responsibility and accountability of employees, and the need for their continual professional development, Argyris and Schon noted that individuals ultimately choose their learning models and the systems they spread throughout their organizations.

SUMMARY

The examples of Machiavelli and Lao-tzu have been used for purposes of clarification and to provoke thoughtful and critical consideration of corporate leadership style. As models, they are admittedly oversimplifications and are best viewed as opposite ends along a continuum. The argument made here is that changing organizational realities in business implies that leadership behavior should progressively incorporate more of the attributes of that Taoist style. The fatal flaw of the extreme Machiavellian model is that the dissonance between what the autocratic leader wants and what it elicits from stakeholders ultimately renders the style counterproductive. The relationship between corporate leadership and employees, as well as owners and other external stakeholders, cannot be adversarial and based on distrust. The autocratic approach is obsolete; it traps the highly educated knowledge worker in an organization that smothers the innovation necessary for long-term competitiveness. Many of the attributes of the Taoist leadership style, on the other hand, speak strongly to the modern business environment, one where the need for swift response to change implies that leadership must be exerted at all levels, where innovative companies rich in new ideas are associated with leaders who empathize strongly with employees, and where "as a leader you actually work for the people who work for you" (Nicholls, 1990, p. 88; Rotemberg, 1993, p. 1318; Belasco and Strayer, 1994, p. 32).

The empowering leader, then, uses his or her position to benefit others and, in return, gains the trust of those who are led. But, using an argument Machiavelli himself employed, won't the reign of a leader who behaves as if the world were as it *ought* to be and not as it *is* (at least to Machiavelli), be short-lived? The Taoist leader's extreme piousness, avoidance of greatness, and unwillingness to compete with others are perhaps not germane to corporate leadership. But many of the attributes of Taoism do reflect the empowering style the dynamic modern business context demands of its leaders: unwavering self confidence, nurturing others instead of dominating or intimidating them, helping them reach their potential, leading by serving.

Citing the turnaround of the Chrylser Corporation, Nicholls has pointed out that there are times even today when autocracy has its place. When the survival of an organization is threatened, it may have to retreat into centralized leadership. But this has become the exception, not the rule. "The benefits of leadership initiatives," writes Nicholls (1990, p. 87) "... will only be realized if the leader is able to engage with people and liberate their potential rather than attempting to coerce innovative behavior as a controller/manipulator." In a period when economic growth is predicated on a future of highly skilled and self-motivated workers, it is critical that business leaders judge their own leadership effectiveness by their ability to inculcate it within others.

NOTE

It is recognized that the striking differences in historical and cultural contexts of Machiavelli and Lao-tzu impinge upon the leadership styles they espoused. In this paper instead of focusing on these differences in influences, Lao-tzu and Machiavelli are treated as archetypes that transcend time and place, in order to help clarify the empowering and autocratic leadership styles. Studies of leadership models developed by other historical figures suggest that the individual circumstances of the figure, when combined with the effects of time period and culture, render each approach unique. For instance, it appears that the notion that there is a single "Eastern" or "Oriental" approach to management or leadership is misleading. Sun-tzu (*The Art of War*), like Lao-tzu, is Chinese, and lived around 500 B.C. However, his approach to leadership is highly militaristic, whereas that of Lao-tzu is not.

REFERENCES

AACSB (1993) "The Cultivation of Tomorrow's Leaders: Industry's Fundamental Challenge to Management Education." *AACSB Newsline,* 23 (3): 1–3.

Argyris, C. and Schon, D.A. (1978). *Organizational Learning: A Theory in Action Perspective.* Reading, MA: Addison-Wesley.

Belasco, J.A. and Stayer, R.C. (1994). "Why Empowerment Doesn't Empower: The Bankruptcy of Current Paradigms," *Business Horizons,* March-April: 31.

Ekvall, G. (1993). "Creativity in Project Work: A Longitudinal Study of a Product Development Project," *Creativity and Innovation Management,* Vol. 2(1): 20.

Huszezo, G.E. (1990). "Training for Team Building." *Training and Development Journal,* February: 37.

Krachenberg, A. R., Henke, J.W., Jr. and Lyons, T.F. (1993). "The Isolation of Upper Management." *Business Horizons.* July-August: 41.

Lao-tzu (circa 531 B.C.). *Tao Te Ching.* Translated by S. Mitchell. New York: Harper Collins Publishers, 1988.

Machiavelli, N. (1531). *The Prince.* 1513. Translated by George Bull. New York: Penguin Books, 1981.

Mintzberg, H. (1984). "Who Should Control the Corporation?" *California Management Review,* Fall: 90–115.

Nicholls, J. (1990). "Rescuing Leadership from Humpty Dumpty." *Journal of General Management,* Winter, Vol. 16, No. 2.

Rotemberg, J.J. and Saloner, G. (1993). "Leadership Style and Incentives." *Management Science,* Vol. 39, No. 11: 1318.

Wriston, W.B. (1990). "The State of American Management," *Harvard Business Review,* Jan-Feb: 79.

MANAGING CHANGE IN BUSINESS:
VIEWS FROM THE ANCIENT PAST

CYNTHIA K. WAGNER

The sentiment was uttered by the ancient Greek thinker, Heraclitus, more than 2,000 years ago: "Everything is born in strife and is in constant flux; and whatever lives, lives by destroying something else." But it could just as easily have been found in any number of recent management treatises. We are, we read, in the midst of the "age of unreason ... an era when change is constant, random," when "what has worked in the past won't work in the future" (Handy, 1989).

The striking parallel between the seemingly archaic realm of ancient philosophy and that of contemporary management should come as no surprise. The nature of change and our role in influencing it and responding to it are, after all, philosophical issues with which humankind has wrestled for more than two millennia. And although Heraclitus' thinking is aligned with the emphasis of modern management literature on continuous change, his beliefs were challenged forcefully in his own era by a trio of Greek thinkers—Parmenides, Plato, and Aristotle—whose arguments remain equally relevant today. Revisiting these counter-arguments brings to the surface some provocative consequences to the assumption that "everything is changing," which contemporary managers would be wise to consider.

This article highlights the viewpoints on change—outlined in Exhibit 1—of Heraclitus and Parmenides, who lived before the seminal Greek thinker, Socrates; and Plato and Aristotle, who followed him. As will become evident, even the simple inquiry "What is change?" opens up a philosophical can of worms. These thinkers offered opposing beliefs as to whether change is real or simply appearance, what causes it, and whether or not it has a purpose. Is it good or bad? What is man's role in change? Does it really even matter? Ancient thought, it turns out, is highly relevant to the management of change in business today. Classical philosophy enriches our approach to change. It affords precedent, provides clarification, and, ironically, offers fresh insight. It forces us to rethink our assumptions and reminds us that the resolution of such philosophical issues as change, even in modern business, is to some degree a matter of perspective—in this case, choosing to emphasize what is changing versus what is not.

THE PRESOCRATICS

The extreme responses to whether or not change exists are represented by Heraclitus and Parmenides. Heraclitus, perhaps best known for his phrase "You cannot step into the same river twice," embraced incessant change.

EXHIBIT I   MANAGING CHANGE: VIEWPOINTS OF FOUR ANCIENT PHILOSOPHERS AND THEIR IMPLICATIONS TO BUSINESS

	Heraclitus (circa 530 to 470 B.C.)	Parmenides (circa 515 to 450 B.C.)	Plato (circa 427 to 347 B.C.)	Aristotle (circa 384 to 322 B.C.)
Existence of Change	Constant change is reality. Stability is illusion.	Reality is stable, permanent. Change is only appearance and is logically impossible.	Change exists, but only in the lower realm of corporeal restlessness, not in the stable, transcendent realm.	Change exists, but is only a manifestation of the temporal world.
Cause of Change	Doctrine of the opposites, in which opposing phases of equal status alternate.	Sense perception, illusion.	Man's cerebral quest for abstract ideals in the upper realm.	Man's attempt to gain what he lacks through actualizing his potential.
Is Change Good?	Yes: the conflict implied by constant change guards against the stagnation of a harmonious world.	No.	No: the world of change is one of degeneration and decay.	No: change means man is lacking in some way.
Does Change Have a Purpose?	No.	No.	Yes: reaching the transcendent nature of pure form.	Yes: the final cause, man's realization of his potential through moral conduct.
Management of Change	Believe only in change. Accept that change is due to chance and necessity. It is purposeless, meaningless, and unmanageable.	Believe only in what is stable, which is discovered through use of reason and logic. Managing change is irrelevant, because change is illusory.	Emphasize stable ideas/forms. Disciplined use of the intellect gives man control over chaos. Only a few superior men will succeed in reaching the changeless world, and these should make decisions for the others.	Emphasize stable ideas/forms. Through reason, contemplation, and observation all people should discover and achieve ideas, i.e., actualize potential. Give change meaning by directing it toward an ultimate goal.
Business Implications	Do not be deluded into thinking stability is possible or desirable. When things seem harmonious, change is on its way. Avoid the stagnation of stability. Accept destruction and loss as a natural part of the process of change.	Do not be deluded into thinking everything is changing. Put thought into maintaining what is stable.	A few select company leaders should establish an unwavering and lofty mission, and rules of conduct to guide the performance of others. Top management alone knows what is best and should set an example for others in the company to follow.	Each person in a company can, through observation and thought, establish goals. They should strive to reach these goals, which benefit not only themselves, but the organization as a whole.

Parmenides, in contrast, presented a radical counterargument that relegated change to illusion. His logical approach to the topic, though not the entire substance of his argument, eventually became a precursor to the thinking of Plato and Aristotle.

HERACLITUS' CONSTANT FLUX

This world ... always was, now is, and shall be—an everlasting fire, catching in measures and going out in measures.

—Heraclitus (from Dye, 1974)

The focus of contemporary management scholars on constant change owes a large debt to Heraclitus, who lived around 500 B.C. His metaphor of fire is apt: "Fire in the first place only lives by consuming and destroying .... [I]t is constantly changing in its material even though it may, like a candle-flame, look steady and permanent enough for awhile" (Guthrie, 1965). To Heraclitus, "All things are in process and nothing stays as it was" (Dye, 1974). Change, and the constant contradiction it implies, are the essence of reality. Moreover, this relentless conflict is good, as it guards against the stagnation of permanence, the death associated with a peaceful and harmonious world. "Through strife all things arise and pass away .... [W]ar is the father and king of all .... [T]he mixture which is not shaken decomposes" (Durant, 1953).

Consider double-digit growth rates in some emerging economies, experimentation in the cloning of human embryos, satellite communication systems that link all corners of the globe, the death of communism in much of Eastern Europe. All seem to bear out Heraclitus' belief that inexorable change alone is reality. Given the plight of AT&T, IBM, the Big Three U.S. auto makers, and countless others, an ever-changing flame would also seem to best represent the chaotic pulse of modern business. As insightful as the claim of constant change appears, however, when it comes to the cause of such change Heraclitus' argument begins to lose its allure. Change, he believed, was caused by the "doctrine of the opposites," in which opposing phases, each with equal status, alternate. In such a world, change has no purpose. A matter of chance and necessity, it occurs simply because that's the way it is. "The states that men regard as differing radically—good and bad, right and wrong, day and night, waking and sleeping, fresh and foul—do not significantly differ when viewed from the perspective of constant change. All, no matter how disparate their properties, are equally episodes in flux" (Dye, 1974).

If, as Heraclitus maintained, "good and ill are the same," it follows that a company's leadership should be unruffled by a sharp change of fortune. IBM can surrender to its competition and chalk it up to "just because," or to the absence of Lady Luck, and take some comfort in knowing that Apple and Microsoft cannot be far behind. Detroit can shrug off the Japanese threat; defeat, after all, is part of the natural process of change. For that matter, Americans in general can stop fretting over the sputtering economic recovery. Where change is constant, a permanent position of global economic leadership is impossible, not to mention boring.

PARMENIDES' SOOTHING STABILITY

Thou canst not know what is not—that is impossible—nor utter it; for it is the same thing that can be thought and that can be.

—Parmenides (from Russell, 1945)

Parmenides refused to step into Heraclitean waters once, much less twice. Change, to him, was a *trompe l'oeil*: simply appearance, temporal. If change alone is reality, he countered, then even speaking truthfully becomes impossible. As soon as one comments on something, it has become something else! Change is a logical contradiction; it requires that what is become something that is not. It is perceived by the senses. Reality, in contrast, is lasting and can only be reached by thought and reason. And reason must prevail.

Parmenides and his followers supported their argument against the absurdity of Heraclitus' fiery flux with a series of paradoxes, some of which are being debated within modern-day philosophical circles. For instance, consider an arrow, seemingly in flight. To Parmenides the arrow is really at rest; at each moment it is simply where it is. A "state of motion" implied by flight—continual change—is inherently contradictory, and thus impossible.

To accept constant change as reality in modern business implies not only the inability to know much about one's company or learn from the past, but also makes "rising and passing away" essentially value-free and beyond control. If change is constant, Parmenides' concern about speaking truthfully would haunt the conscience of any CEO at the annual shareholders' meeting. By the time the company's financial performance, future goals, and mission were uttered, they would no longer be germane. The standards by which performance is measured would become meaningless. Moreover, if, as Heraclitus maintained, "the sun is new every day," the past—and the highly touted experience curve—would be irrelevant.

AFTER SOCRATES

Plato and Aristotle would probably be the first to admit that businesses lulled into Parmenides' stability would likely go the way of the Parthenon. However, their concern with the assumption that "everything is changing" would remain. Though both conceded that change existed, it was not, as Heraclitus advanced, synonymous with reality. They therefore retreated from Parmenides' assertion that change was all in our heads, but also clearly saw implications in the Heraclitean constant flux they could not accept.

PLATO'S TWO WORLDS

The idea of Good, the principle of realizing at all times a maximum of positive value, is the ideal, which offers to mankind the most promising guidance in meeting concrete problems set by an environment in which change appears to be the rule.

—Plato (from Lodge, 1956)

Like Parmenides, Plato believed that Heraclitus' constant flux would empty life of meaning and make any knowledge of the sensible world impossible. Rupert Clendon Lodge, in *The Philosophy of Plato*, states:

When Plato faces the phenomenon of a changing world, in which human organisms, like all other organisms, seem destined to be swept along blindly, as part of the flotsam and jetsam of events inherently devoid of meaning, he refuses to draw the first and most obvious conclusion. Unlike Homer and his fellow Poets, Plato refuses to preach the transitoriness of cultures, the futility of human effort.

And yet Plato also admitted the irrefutable evidence that change exists. To reconcile his recognition of pervasive change with his unwillingness to abandon the possibility of knowledge and meaning, Plato proposed the existence of two distinct worlds, one of corporeal restlessness and the other of unchanging ideas. In the lower world of change, only cloudy opinions, flawed and ephemeral representations of the truth, are possible. Knowledge—apprehension of what does not change—is possible in the upper world, which transcends humans, but to which they can be awakened through a life of intellectual and moral self-discipline.

The cause of change for Plato is humankind's cerebral quest for the immutable, transcendent forms, which gives us control over the chaos and decay below and which guides us in solving the concrete problems of the transient world. The demanding task required to apprehend the ideal forms and thus reach the upper world suggests that only a select few will succeed. And these few alone, according to Plato, should make decisions for the others. Plato's abstract forms provide managerial guidance by establishing lofty standards of conduct. Although achieving these ideals requires extraordinary effort, they provide a lasting sense of mission. What in modern business transcends the flux? Hewlett-Packard's leading-edge technology, Motorola's innovativeness, Southwest Airline's unique combination of customer service and low price, Procter & Gamble's commitment to environmental consciousness—to name a few—represent such transcendence.

Plato's top-down manager of change would resemble a benevolent dictator who spends hours on end scouring the literature, but who seldom ventures from the penthouse suite. Aloof, the Platonic leader alone would, through superior intellectual capacity, know what is best for the company and be a symbol of the company's abiding principles, its ideals.

ARISTOTLE'S TELEOLOGICAL APPROACH

A thing changes over time but it continues to be its essence, which at any moment is represented by its actualized and its unactualized potentialities, namely, the thing itself.

—Aristotle (from Koutougos, 1977)

Aristotle, too, accepted that change exists. According to Allan (1970), he thought Parmenides' stubborn refusal to concede this had retarded the progress of science. Like Plato, however, Aristotle chose to emphasize what remains stable over what does not. To him, change was no more than an imperfect manifestation of the temporal world: "If man needs change, it is because he is lacking in some way" (Anton and Kustas, 1971). What man lacks he should try to gain, via what Aristotle calls actualizing his potential, which is the cause of change. In the final destination of our actualization, we will find stability and permanence. Aristotle's focus is not on the process of coming to be, but on the ultimate goal of change. Managing change requires that we know what it is directed toward, its purpose. Change itself is meaningless unless it is guided by the goals we establish.

Our ultimate goal—the "final cause," to Aristotle—is to realize our potential through moral conduct, reason, philosophy, and contemplation. Aristotle believed in the role of ideal forms in guiding decision-making, as did his mentor. However, unlike Plato, who allowed that only a very few people would have the intellectual wherewithal and desire to establish and reach the ideals and thus manage change, Aristotle's process of actualization is open to anyone willing to think and observe. His guiding forms do not exist in Plato's abstract transcendent realm, but in man himself. Moreover, his goal is not Platonic knowledge of principles, but the practice of these principles. One can imagine the Aristotelian manager pacing around on the shop floor, sleeves rolled to the elbows, a master communicator, engaging anyone willing in a lively discussion of where the company should be headed. A strong proponent of participatory decision-making, he would constantly empower employees by encouraging input from his workers and management. Together they would find ways to reach their own potential as they work to achieve what is best for the organization as a whole.

> From Socrates' standpoint, it is better, always better, to be reflective, critically reflective: aware of high standards and dissatisfied with one's actual achievements. It is unworthy of a human being to remain unreflective, uncritically satisfied with a life like that of a pig, however gregarious. (Lodge, 1956)

The danger in popularizing a notion such as change is that it may be trivialized. As important as the topic has become to the climate of opinion in modern business, we need to avoid the temptation of believing that a philosophical argument with ancient roots has at last been resolved. The purpose in bringing to light the multifaceted approaches to change offered by ancient thinkers has been to keep us out of the pen to which Socrates referred.

How, then, do these varied and contrasting viewpoints inform our understanding and management of change in relation to business today? That companies are mindless pawns in a chaotic world is, of course, ludicrous. However, as Parmenides, Plato, and Aristotle have demonstrated, this scenario follows quite logically from the assumption that "everything is changing." Neither Plato nor Aristotle supports Parmenides' denial of change; instead, they offer distinct yet compatible alternatives to surrendering to the "triumph of the Heraclitean flux" (Tarnas, 1991). What Plato and Aristotle say to modern managers is that we must surely recognize change along various fronts—technological, economic, social, and political. Managing change, however, means that instead of being unwittingly pulled into the vortex, we need to focus on what supersedes it.

The Platonic approach places the burden of managing change squarely on the shoulders of leaders, who must constantly emphasize the company's values and ideals—the fundamental reasons an organization exists, which do not waver. These might be expressed in the firm's mission statement; but, more important, the values and ideals must be embodied in the behavior of its leaders, who serve as examples to the rest of the organization. Leadership becomes a symbol of what remains stable despite what appears to be incessant change in the company's environment and internal operations. Visionary leadership, then, appears to have its roots in Plato.

Aristotle's approach to managing change implies that the establishment of long-term goals, and the process of striving to reach these goals, are key to maintaining an organization's stability. This process is not only the responsibility of company leadership; empowerment is Aristotle's legacy. Involving everyone in the organization in setting and attaining goals ensures that the objectives of individuals are consonant with those of the company as a whole, and employees should be chosen and rewarded on this basis.

Change, then, is *not* all in our heads, as Parmenides insisted. However, our willingness and ability to manage it are. As Heraclitus maintained, change may have no intrinsic meaning. We give it meaning by harnessing it: by guiding it with our values and ideals—toward our ends—as opposed to viewing it as an inexorable process over which we have no control.

REFERENCES

Allan, D.J. (1970). *The Philosophy of Aristotle.* London: Oxford University Press.
Anton, J.P. and Kustas, G.L. (1971). *Essays in Ancient Greek Philosophy.* Albany: State University of New York Press.
Brumbaugh, R.S. (1964). *The Philosophers of Greece.* New York: Crowell.
Durant, W. (1953). *The Story of Philosophy.* New York: Simon and Schuster.
Dye, J.W. (1974). "Heraclitus and the Future of Process Philosophy," *Tulane Studies in Philosophy.* 23: 1331.
Guthrie, W.K.C. (1960). *The Greek Philosophers.* New York: Harper.
Guthrie, W.K.C. (1965). *A History of Greek Philosophy, Vol. 1.* London: Cambridge University Press.
Handy, C. (1989). *The Age of Unreason.* Boston: Harvard Business School Press.
Koutougos, A. (1977). "The Relevancy of Aristotle's Theory of Change to Modern Issues," *Philosphia* (Athens). 7: 315–322.
Lodge, R.C. (1956). *The Philosophy of Plato.* London: Routledge & Kegan Paul, Ltd.
Russell, B. (1945). *A History of Western Philosophy.* New York: Simon and Schuster.
Tarnas, R. (1991). *The Passion of the Western Mind.* New York: Harmony Books.

QUESTIONS: SECTION THREE

WOULD YOU WANT MACHIAVELLI AS YOUR CEO?
CYNTHIA K. WAGNER

1. Is the Machiavellian approach more appropriate to certain company types or business conditions?

2. What are the long-term implications of *The Prince*'s approach to strategy? How will employees, shareholders, and the government react?

3. Are there modern-day examples of strategists aligned with Machiavelli? Has the approach worked? Are there modern-day examples of strategists aligned with Lao-tzu? Has the approach worked?

4. Would you prefer to work under a Machiavellian or Taoist leader—or someone with characteristics of both? As a leader, would you prefer to take the approach of Machiavelli or Lao-tzu or a combination of both?

MANAGING CHANGE IN BUSINESS: VIEWS FROM THE ANCIENT PAST
CYNTHIA K. WAGNER

1. Is "everything" changing? What does this really mean?

2. What in business strategy might not change? Are there examples of elements of strategy in actual companies that have not changed, even during times of rapid change in the environment?

3. Is Plato's approach to managing change more appropriate in some conditions or company types versus others? Is Aristotle's approach to managing change more appropriate in some conditions or company types versus others?

4

Roads Less Traveled

What is the right way to manage creativity in the interests of heightened strategic insight?
Look at the sheet music in your organization, and then feel free to throw it away.

—John Kao (1997)

The articles in the fourth part of our journey are among the most unusual in the collection. They take us into new territory, and provoke novel ways of thinking and modes of expression. "The Origin of Strategy" applies concepts of evolutionary biology to strategic management. The second article, "Crafting Strategy," draws lessons in strategic management from pottery-making. Finally, "Strategic Decisions and All That Jazz" uses musical improvisation as a metaphor for explaining the way strategy is accomplished in dynamic high-technology companies.

In the first selection Bruce Henderson, former head of the Boston Consulting Group, uses evolution to describe a strategy for gaining advantage in the marketplace. He finds Darwin's theory of evolution much superior to economic theory in understanding business competition. Henderson argues that the ubiquitous concept of market share is meaningless, because it depends upon how narrowly or broadly a company arbitrarily defines its market. A fundamental tenet of Darwinism, Gause's principle demonstrates that competitors only survive when they have something different enough to give them a natural advantage. Henderson therefore believes that companies should begin by defining the segment of market they monopolize and work from there, by enlarging the scope of the company's advantage. "Move the boundary of advantage into the competitor's market and keep them from doing the same." It is through strategy that we "plan for evolution." Strategy—made possible by the unique human powers of imagination and logical reasoning—allows us to speed up the processes of competition and change.

"Managers are craftsmen and strategy is their clay," argues Henry Mintzberg in *Crafting Strategy*. Mintzberg's metaphor is a fertile source of insight into strategic management. Like the craftsman, managers must know their materials thoroughly. They must have an overall sense of design, yet be able to detect when a change in direction is in order. Sometimes these changes are radical and require reconstitution of a company's higher-level objectives, its major policies, and perhaps even its overriding mission. Other times, the company's umbrella strategy remains in place and only programmatic changes are necessary. Just as successful potters tightly couple thought and action, strategists must integrate the processes of formulation and implementation. Separating them, Mintzberg warns, inevitably results in a loss of connection between what the strategist envisions and what actually happens. The strategist loses the ability to learn.

In the third article Kathleen Eisenhardt borrows lessons in strategy from the likes of music greats Miles Davis and Dave Brubeck. Jazz improvisation, according to Eisenhardt, overcomes the weaknesses of models of strategy based on bounded rationality, power and politics, and purely random decision-making. Strategists in fast paced and highly competitive industries find improvisation works because it relies on intense communication within top management teams, and rules that are few in number, but strictly adhered to.

THE ORIGIN OF STRATEGY

BRUCE D. HENDERSON

Consider this lesson in strategy. In 1934, Professor G.F. Gause of Moscow University, known as "the father of mathematical biology," published the results of a set of experiments in which he put two very small animals (protozoans) of the same genus in a bottle with an adequate supply of food. If the animals were of different species, they could survive and persist together. If they were of the same species, they could not. This observation led to Gause's Principle of Competitive Exclusion: No two species can coexist that make their living in the identical way.

Competition existed long before strategy. It began with life itself. The first one-cell organisms required certain resources to maintain life. When these resources were adequate, the number grew from one generation to the next. As life evolved, these organisms became a resource for more complex forms of life, and so on up the food chain. When any pair of species competed for some essential resource, sooner or later one displaced the other. In the absence of counterbalancing forces that could maintain a stable equilibrium by giving each species an advantage in its own territory, only one of any pair survived.

Over millions of years, a complex network of competitive interaction developed. Today more than a million distinct existing species have been cataloged, each with some unique advantage in competing for the resources it requires. (There are thought to be millions more as yet unclassified.) At any given time, thousands of species are becoming extinct and thousands more are emerging.

What explains this abundance? Variety. The richer the environment, the greater the number of potentially significant variables that can give each species a unique advantage. But also, the richer the environment, the greater the potential number of competitors—and the more severe the competition.

For millions of years, natural competition involved no strategy. By chance and the laws of probability, competitors found the combinations of resources that best matched their different characteristics. This was not strategy but Darwinian natural selection, based on adaptation and the survival of the fittest. The same pattern exists in all living systems, including business.

In both the competition of the ecosphere and the competition of trade and commerce, random chance is probably the major, all-pervasive factor. Chance determines the mutations and variations that survive and thrive from generation to generation. Those that leave relatively fewer offspring are displaced. Those that adapt best displace the rest. Physical and structural characteristics evolve and adapt to match the competitive environment. Behavior patterns evolve too and become embedded as instinctual reactions.

Reprinted by permission of *Harvard Business Review*. From "The Origin of Strategy," by Bruce D. Henderson, Nov-Dec, 1989: 139–143. Copyright © 1989 by the Harvard Business School Publishing Corporation; all rights reserved.

In fact, business and biological competition would follow the same pattern of gradual evolutionary change except for one thing. Business strategists can use their imagination and ability to reason logically to accelerate the effects of competition and the rate of change. In other words, imagination and logic make strategy possible. Without them, behavior and tactics are either intuitive or the result of conditioned reflexes. But imagination and logic are only two of the factors that determine shifts in competitive equilibrium. Strategy also requires the ability to understand the complex web of natural competition.

If every business could grow indefinitely, the total market would grow to an infinite size on a finite earth. It has never happened. Competitors perpetually crowd each other out. The fittest survive and prosper until they displace their competitors or outgrow their resources. What explains this evolutionary process? Why do business competitors achieve the equilibrium they do?

Remember Gause's Principle. Competitors that make their living in the same way cannot coexist—no more in business than in nature. Each must be different enough to have a unique advantage. The continued existence of a number of competitors is proof per se that their advantages over each other are mutually exclusive. They may look alike, but they are different species.

Consider Sears, K-Mart, Wal-Mart, and Radio Shack. These stores overlap in the merchandise they sell, in the customers they serve, and in the areas where they operate. But to survive, each of these retailers has had to differentiate itself in important ways, to dominate different segments of the market. Each sells to different customers or offers different values, services, or products.

What differentiates competitors in business may be purchase price, function, time utility (the difference between instant gratification and "someday, as soon as possible"), or place utility (when your heating and cooling system quits, the manufacturer's technical expert is not nearly as valuable as the local mechanic). Or it may be nothing but the customer's perception of the product and its supplier. Indeed, image is often the only basis of comparison between similar but different alternatives. That is why advertising can be valuable.

Since businesses can combine these factors in many different ways, there will always be many possibilities for competitive coexistence. But also, many possibilities for each competitor exist to enlarge the scope of its advantage by changing what differentiates it from its rivals. Can evolution be planned for in business? That is what strategy is for.

Strategy is a deliberate search for a plan of action that will develop a business's competitive advantage and compound it. For any company, the search is an iterative process that begins with a recognition of where you are and what you have now. Your most dangerous competitors are those that are most like you. The differences between you and your competitors are the basis of your advantage. If you are in business and are self-supporting, you already have some kind of competitive advantage, no matter how small or subtle. Otherwise, you would have gradually lost customers faster than you gained them. The objective is to enlarge the scope of your advantage, which can happen only at someone else's expense.

Chasing market share is almost as productive as chasing the pot of gold at the end of the rainbow. You can never get there. Even if you could, you would find nothing. If you are in business, you already have 100% of your own market. So do your competitors. Your real goal is to expand the size of your market. But you will always have 100% of your market, whether it grows or shrinks.

Your present market is what, where, and to whom you are selling what you now sell. Survival depends on keeping 100% of this market. To grow and prosper, however, you must expand the market in which you can maintain an advantage over any and all competitors who might be selling to your customers.

Unless a business has a unique advantage over its rivals, it has no reason to exist. Unfortunately, many businesses compete in important areas where they operate at a disadvantage—often at great cost, until, inevitably, they are crowded out. That happened to Texas Instruments and its pioneering personal computer. TI invented the semiconductor; its business was built on instrumentation. Why was it forced out of the personal computer business?

Many executives have been led on a wild goose chase after market share by their inability to define the potential market in which they would, or could, enjoy a competitive advantage. Remember the Edsel? And the Mustang? Xerox invented the copying machine; why couldn't IBM become a major competitor in this field? What did Kodak do to virtually dominate the large-scale business copier market in the United States? What did Coca-Cola do to virtually dominate the soft drink business in Japan?

But what is market share? Grape Nuts has 100% of the Grape Nuts market, a smaller percentage of the breakfast cereal market, an even smaller percentage of the packaged-foods market, a still smaller percentage of the packaged-goods shelf-space market, a tiny percentage of the U.S. food market, a minuscule percentage of the world food market, and a microscopic percentage of total consumer expenditures.

Market share is a meaningless number unless a company defines the market in terms of the boundaries separating it from its rivals. These boundaries are the points at which the company and a particular competitor are equivalent in a potential customer's eyes. The trick lies in moving the boundary of advantage into the potential competitor's market and keeping that competitor from doing the same. The competitor that truly has an advantage can give potential customers more for their money and still have a larger margin between its cost and its selling price. That extra can be converted into either growth or larger payouts to the business's owners.

So what is new? The marketing wars are forever. But market share is malarkey.

Strategic competition compresses time. Competitive shifts that might take generations to evolve instead occur in a few short years. Strategic competition is not new, of course. Its elements have been recognized and used ever since humans combined intelligence, imagination, accumulated resources, and coordinated behavior to wage war. But strategic competition in business is a relatively recent phenomenon. It may well have as profound an impact on business productivity as the industrial revolution had on individual productivity.

The basic elements of strategic competition are these: (1) ability to understand competitive behavior as a system in which competitors, customers, money, people, and resources continually interact; (2) ability to use this understanding to predict how a given strategic move will rebalance the competitive equilibrium; (3) resources that can be permanently committed to new uses even though the benefits will be deferred; (4) ability to predict risk and return with enough accuracy and confidence to justify that commitment; and (5) willingness to act.

This list may sound like nothing more than the basic requirements for making any ordinary investment. But strategy is not that simple. It is all-encompassing, calling on the commitment and dedication of the whole organization. Any competitor's failure to react and then deploy and commit its own resources against the strategic move of a rival can turn existing competitive relationships upside down. That is why strategic competition compresses time. Natural competition has none of these characteristics.

Natural competition is wildly expedient in its moment-to-moment interaction. But it is inherently conservative in the way it changes a species's characteristic behavior. By contrast, strategic commitment is deliberate, carefully considered, and tightly reasoned. But the consequences may well be radical change in a relatively short period of time. Natural competition is evolutionary. Strategic competition is revolutionary.

Natural competition works by a process of low risk, incremental trial and error. Small changes are tried and tested. Those that are beneficial are gradually adopted and maintained. No need for foresight or commitment, what matters is adaptation to the way things are now. Natural competition can and does evolve exquisitely complex and effective forms eventually. Humans are just such an end result. But unmanaged change takes thousands of generations. Often it cannot keep up with a fast-changing environment and with the adaptation of competitors.

By committing resources, strategy seeks to make sweeping changes in competitive relationships. Only two fundamental inhibitions moderate its revolutionary character. One is failure, which can be as far-reaching in its consequences as success. The other is the inherent advantage that an alert defender has over an attacker. Success usually depends on the culture, perceptions, attitudes, and characteristic behavior of competitors and on their mutual awareness of each other.

This is why, in geopolitics and military affairs as well as in business, long periods of equilibrium are punctuated by sharp shifts in competitive relationships. It is the age-old pattern of war and peace and then war again. Natural competition continues during periods of peace. In business, however, peace is becoming increasingly rare. When an aggressive competitor launches a successful strategy, all the other businesses with which it competes must respond with equal foresight and dedication of resources.

In 1975, the British War Office opened its classified files on World War II. Serious readers of these descriptions of "war by other means" may feel inclined to revise their thinking about what happened in that war and about strategy generally, particularly the differences between actual strategies and apparent strategies.

The evidence is clear that the outcome of individual battles and campaigns often depended on highly subjective evaluations of the combatants' intentions, capabilities, and behavior. But until the records were unsealed, only people who were directly involved appreciated this. Historians and other observers ascribed victories and defeats to grand military plans or chance.

Also in 1975, Edward O. Wilson published *Sociobiology*, a landmark study in which he tried to synthesize all that is known about population biology, zoology, genetics, and animal behavior. What emerged was a framework for understanding the success of species in terms of social behavior—that is, competition for resources. This synthesis is the closest approach to a general theory of competition that I know of. It provides abundant parallels for business behavior as well as for the economic competition that characterizes our own species.

Human beings may be at the top of the ecological chain, but we are still members of the ecological community. That is why Darwin is probably a better guide to business competition than economists are.

Classical economic theories of business competition are so simplistic and sterile that they have been less contributions to understanding than obstacles. These theories postulate rational, self-interested behavior by individuals who interact through market exchanges in a fixed and static legal system of property and contracts. Their frame of reference is "perfect competition," a theoretical abstraction that never has existed and never could exist.

In contrast, Charles Darwin's *On the Origin of Species*, published in 1859, outlines a more fruitful perspective and point of departure for developing business strategy: "Some make the deep-seated error of considering the physical conditions of a country as the most important for its inhabitants; whereas it cannot, I think, be disputed that the nature of the other inhabitants with which each has to compete is generally a far more important element of success."

CRAFTING STRATEGY

HENRY MINTZBERG

Imagine someone planning strategy. What likely springs to mind is an image of orderly thinking: a senior manager, or a group of them, sitting in an office formulating courses of action that everyone else will implement on schedule. The keynote is reason—rational control, the systematic analysis of competitors and markets, of company strengths and weaknesses, the combination of these analyses producing clear, explicit, full-blown strategies.

Now imagine someone crafting strategy. A wholly different image likely results, as different from planning as craft is from mechanization. Craft evokes traditional skill, dedication, perfection through the mastery of detail. What springs to mind is not so much thinking and reason as involvement, a feeling of intimacy and harmony with the materials at hand, developed through long experience and commitment. Formulation and implementation merge into a fluid process of learning through which creative strategies evolve.

My thesis is simple: the crafting image better captures the process by which effective strategies come to be. The planning image, long popular in the literature, distorts these processes and thereby misguides organizations that embrace it unreservedly.

In developing this thesis, I shall draw on the experiences of a single craftsman, a potter, and compare them with the results of a research project that tracked the strategies of a number of corporations across several decades. Because the two contexts are so obviously different, my metaphor, like my assertion, may seem farfetched at first. Yet, if we think of a craftsman as an organization of one, we can see that he or she must also resolve one of the great challenges the corporate strategist faces: knowing the organization's capabilities well enough to think deeply enough about its strategic direction. By considering strategy-making from the perspective of one person, free of all the paraphernalia of what has been called the strategy industry, we can learn something about the formation of strategy in the corporation. For much as our potter has to manage her craft, so too managers have to craft their strategy.

At work, the potter sits before a lump of clay on the wheel. Her mind is on the clay, but she is also aware of sitting between her past experiences and her future prospects. She knows exactly what has and has not worked for her in the past. She has an intimate knowledge of her work, her capabilities, and her markets. As a craftsman, she senses rather than analyzes these things; her knowledge is "tacit." All these things are working in her mind as her hands are working the clay. The product that emerges on the wheel is likely to be in the tradition of her past work, but she may break away and embark on a new direction. Even so, the past is no less present, projecting itself into the future.

In my metaphor, managers are craftsmen and strategy is their clay. Like the potter, they sit between a past of corporate capabilities and a future of market opportunities. And if they are truly craftsmen, they bring to their work an equally intimate knowledge of the materials at hand. That is the essence of crafting strategy.

In the pages that follow, we will explore this metaphor by looking at how strategies get made as opposed to how they are supposed to get made. Throughout, I will be drawing on the two sets of experiences I've mentioned. One is a research project on patterns in strategy formation that has been going on at McGill University under my direction since 1971. The second is the stream of work of a successful potter, my wife, who began her craft in 1967.

Ask almost anyone what strategy is, and they will define it as a plan of some sort, an explicit guide to future behavior. Then ask them what strategy a competitor or a government or even they themselves have actually pursued. Chances are they will describe consistency in *past* behavior—a pattern in action over time. Strategy, it turns out, is one of those words that people define in one way and often use in another, without realizing the difference.

The reason for this is simple. Strategy's formal definition and its Greek military origins notwithstanding, we need the word as much to explain past actions as to describe intended behavior. After all, if strategies can be planned and intended, they can also be pursued and realized (or not realized, as the case may be). And pattern in action, or what we call realized strategy, explains that pursuit. Moreover, just as a plan need not produce a pattern (some strategies that are intended are simply not realized), so too a pattern need not result from a plan. An organization can have a pattern (or realized strategy) without knowing it, let alone making it explicit.

Patterns, like beauty, are in the mind of the beholder, of course. But anyone reviewing a chronological lineup of our craftsman's work would have little trouble discerning clear patterns, at least in certain periods. Until 1974, for example, she made small, decorative ceramic animals and objects of various kinds. Then this "knickknack strategy" stopped abruptly, and eventually new patterns formed around wafer-like sculptures and ceramic bowls, highly textured and unglazed.

Finding equivalent patterns in action for organizations isn't that much more difficult. Indeed, for such large companies as Volkswagenwerk and Air Canada, in our research, it proved simpler! (As well it should. A craftsman, after all, can change what she does in a studio a lot more easily than a Volkswagenwerk can retool its assembly lines.) Mapping the product models at Volkswagenwerk from the late 1940s to the late 1970s, for example, uncovers a clear pattern of concentration on the Beetle, followed in the late 1960s by a frantic search for replacements through acquisitions and internally developed new models, to a strategic reorientation around more stylish, watercooled, front wheel-drive vehicles in the mid-1970s.

But what about intended strategies, those formal plans and pronouncements we think of when we use the term *strategy*? Ironically, here we run into all kinds of problems. Even with a single craftsman, how can we know what her intended strategies really were? If we could go back, would we find expressions of intention? And if we could, would we be able to trust them? We often fool ourselves, as well as others, by denying our subconscious motives. And remember that intentions are cheap, at least when compared with realizations.

READING THE ORGANIZATION'S MIND

If you believe all this has more to do with the Freudian recesses of a craftsman's mind than with the practical realities of producing automobiles, then think again. For who knows what the intended strategies of a Volkswagenwerk really mean, let alone what they are? Can we simply assume in this collective context that the company's intended strategies are represented by its formal plans or by other statements emanating from the executive suite? Might these be just vain hopes or rationalizations or ploys to fool the competition? And even if expressed intentions exist, to what extent do others in the organization share them? How do we read the collective mind? Who is the strategist anyway?

The traditional view of strategic management resolves these problems quite simply, by what organizational theorists call attribution. You see it all the time in the business press. When General Motors acts, it's because Roger Smith has made a strategy. Given realization, there must have been intention, and that is automatically attributed to the chief.

In a short magazine article, this assumption is understandable. Journalists don't have a lot of time to uncover the origins of strategy, and GM is a large, complicated organization. But just consider all the complexity and confusion that gets tucked under this assumption—all the meetings and debates, the many people, the dead ends, the folding and unfolding of ideas. Now imagine trying to build a formal strategy-making system around that assumption. Is it any wonder that formal strategic planning is often such a resounding failure?

To unravel some of the confusion—and move away from the artificial complexity we have piled around the strategy-making process—we need to get back to some basic concepts. The most basic of all is the intimate connection between thought and action. That is the key to craft, and so also to the crafting of strategy.

Virtually everything that has been written about strategy-making depicts it as a deliberate process. First we think, then we act. We formulate, then we implement. The progression seems so perfectly sensible. Why would anybody want to proceed differently?

Our potter is in the studio, rolling the clay to make a wafer-like sculpture. The clay sticks to the rolling pin, and a round form appears. Why not make a cylindrical vase? One idea leads to another, until a new pattern forms. Action has driven thinking: a strategy has emerged.

Out in the field, a salesman visits a customer. The product isn't quite right, and together they work out some modifications. The salesman returns to his company and puts the changes through; after two or three more rounds, they finally get it right. A new product emerges, which eventually opens up a new market. The company has changed strategic course.

In fact, most salespeople are less fortunate than this one or than our craftsman. In an organization of one, the implementer is the formulator, so innovations can be incorporated into strategy quickly and easily. In a large organization, the innovator may be ten levels removed from the leader who is supposed to dictate strategy and may also have to sell the idea to dozens of peers doing the same job.

Some salespeople, of course, can proceed on their own, modifying products to suit their customers and convincing skunk works in the factory to produce them. In effect, they pursue their own strategies. Maybe no one else notices or cares. Sometimes, however, their innovations do get noticed, perhaps years later, when the company's prevalent strategies have broken down and its leaders are groping for something new. Then, the salesperson's strategy may be allowed to pervade the system, to become organizational.

Is this story farfetched? Certainly not. We've all heard stories like it. But since we tend to see only what we believe, if we believe that strategies have to be planned, we're unlikely to see the real meaning such stories hold.

Consider how the National Film Board of Canada (NFB) came to adopt a feature-film strategy. The NFB is a federal government agency, famous for its creativity, and expert in the production of short documentaries. Some years back, it funded a filmmaker on a project that unexpectedly ran long. To distribute his film, the NFB turned to theaters and so inadvertently gained experience in marketing feature-length films. Other filmmakers caught onto the idea, and eventually the NFB found itself pursuing a feature film strategy—a pattern of producing such films.

My point is simple, deceptively simple: strategies can form as well as be *formulated*. A realized strategy can emerge in response to an evolving situation, or it can be brought about deliberately, through a process of formulation followed by implementation. But when these planned intentions do not produce the desired actions, organizations are left with unrealized strategies.

Today we hear a great deal about unrealized strategies, almost always in concert with the claim that implementation has failed. Management has been lax, controls have been loose, people haven't been committed. Excuses abound. At times, indeed, they may be valid. But often these explanations prove too easy. So some people look beyond implementation to formulation. The strategists haven't been smart enough.

While it is certainly true that many intended strategies are ill conceived, I believe that the problem often lies one step beyond, in the distinction we make between formulation and implementation, the common assumption that thought must be independent of (and precede) action. Sure, people could be smarter—but not only by conceiving more clever strategies. Sometimes they can be smarter by allowing their strategies to develop gradually, through the organization's actions and experiences. Smart strategists appreciate that they cannot always be smart enough to think through everything in advance.

HANDS & MINDS

No craftsman thinks some days and works others. The craftsman's mind is going constantly, in tandem with her hands. Yet large organizations try to separate the work of minds and hands. In so doing, they often sever the vital feedback link between the two. The salesperson who finds a customer with an unmet need may possess the most strategic bit of information in the entire organization. But that information is useless if he or she cannot create a strategy in response to it or else convey the information to someone who can—because the channels are blocked or because the formulators have simply finished formulating. The notion that strategy is something that should happen way up there, far removed from the details of running an organization on a daily basis, is one of the great fallacies of conventional strategic management. And it explains a good many of the most dramatic failures in business and public policy today.

We at McGill call strategies like the NFB's that appear without clear intentions—or in spite of them—emergent strategies. Actions simply converge into patterns. They may become deliberate, of course, if the pattern is recognized and then legitimated by senior management. But that's after the fact.

All this may sound rather strange, I know. Strategies that emerge? Managers who acknowledge strategies already formed? Over the years, our research group at McGill has met with a good deal of resistance from people upset by what they perceive to be our passive definition of a word so bound up with proactive behavior and free will. After all, strategy means control—the ancient Greeks used it to describe the art of the army general.

STRATEGIC LEARNING

But we have persisted in this usage for one reason: learning. Purely deliberate strategy precludes learning once the strategy is formulated; emergent strategy fosters it. People take actions one by one and respond to them, so that patterns eventually form.

Our craftsman tries to make a freestanding sculptural form. It doesn't work, so she rounds it a bit here, flattens it a bit there. The result looks better, but still isn't quite right. She makes another and another and another. Eventually, after days or months or years, she finally has what she wants. She is off on a new strategy.

In practice, of course, all strategy-making walks on two feet, one deliberate, the other emergent. For just as purely deliberate strategy-making precludes learning, so purely emergent strategy-making precludes control. Pushed to the limit, neither approach makes much sense. Learning must be coupled with control. That is why the McGill research group uses the word strategy for both emergent and deliberate behavior.

Likewise, there is no such thing as a purely deliberate strategy or a purely emergent one. No organization—not even the ones commanded by those ancient Greek generals—knows enough to work everything out in advance, to ignore learning en route. And no one—not even a solitary potter—can be flexible enough to leave everything to happenstance, to give up all control. Craft requires control just as it requires responsiveness to the material at hand. Thus deliberate and emergent strategy form the end points of a continuum along which the strategies that are crafted in the real world may be found. Some strategies may approach either end, but many more fall at intermediate points.

Effective strategies can show up in the strangest places and develop through the most unexpected means. There is no one best way to make strategy.

The form for a cat collapses on the wheel, and our potter sees a bull taking shape. Clay sticks to a rolling pin, and a line of cylinders results. Wafers come into being because of a shortage of clay and limited kiln space in a studio in France. Thus errors become opportunities, and limitations stimulate creativity. The natural propensity to experiment, even boredom, likewise stimulate strategic change.

Organizations that craft their strategies have similar experiences. Recall the National Film Board with its inadvertently long film. Or consider its experiences with experimental films, which made special use of animation and sound. For 20 years, the NFB produced a bare but steady trickle of such films. In fact, every film but one in that trickle was produced by a single person, Norman McLaren, the NFB's most celebrated filmmaker. McLaren pursued a personal strategy of experimentation, deliberate for him perhaps (though who can know whether he had the whole stream in mind or simply planned one film at a time?) but not for the organization. Then 20 years later, others followed his lead and the trickle widened, his *personal strategy* becoming more broadly organizational.

Conversely, in 1952, when television came to Canada, a *consensus strategy* quickly emerged at the NFB. Senior management was not keen on producing films for the new medium. But while the arguments raged, one filmmaker quietly went off and made a single series for TV. That precedent set, one by one his colleagues leapt in, and within months the NFB—and its management—found themselves committed for several years to a new strategy with an intensity unmatched before or since. This consensus strategy arose spontaneously, as a result of many independent decisions made by the filmmakers about the films they wished to make. Can we call this strategy deliberate? For the filmmakers perhaps; for senior management certainly not. But for the organization? It all depends on your perspective, on how you choose to read the organization's mind.

While the NFB may seem like an extreme case, it highlights behavior that can be found, albeit in muted form, in all organizations. Those who doubt this might read Richard Pascale's account of how Honda stumbled into its enormous success in the American motorcycle market. Brilliant as its strategy may have looked after the fact, Honda's managers made almost every conceivable mistake until the market finally hit them over the head with the right formula. The Honda managers on site in America, driving their products themselves (and thus inadvertently picking up market reaction), did only one thing right: they learned, firsthand (Pascale, 1984).

GRASS-ROOTS STRATEGY-MAKING

These strategies all reflect, in whole or part, what we like to call a grass-roots approach to strategic management. Strategies grow like weeds in a garden. They take root in all kinds of places, wherever people have the capacity to learn (because they are in touch with the situation) and the resources to support that capacity. These strategies become organizational when they become collective, that is, when they proliferate to guide the behavior of the organization at large.

Of course, this view is overstated. But it is no less extreme than the conventional view of strategic management, which might be labeled the hothouse approach. Neither is right. Reality falls between the two. Some of the most effective strategies we uncovered in our research combined deliberation and control with flexibility and organizational learning.

Consider first what we call the *umbrella strategy*. Here senior management sets out broad guidelines (say, to produce only high-margin products at the cutting edge of technology or to favor products using bonding technology) and leaves the specifics (such as what these products will be) to others lower down in the organization. This strategy is not only deliberate (in its guidelines) and emergent (in its specifics), but it is also deliberately emergent in that the process is consciously managed to allow strategies to emerge en route. IBM used the umbrella strategy in the early 1960s with the impending 360 series, when its senior management approved a set of broad criteria for the design of a family of computers later developed in detail throughout the organization (Quinn, 1988).

Deliberately emergent, too, is what we call the *process strategy*. Here management controls the process of strategy formation—concerning itself with the design of the structure, its staffing, procedures, and so on—while leaving the actual content to others. Both process and umbrella strategies seem to be especially prevalent in businesses that require great expertise and creativity—a 3M, a Hewlett-Packard, a National Film Board. Such organizations can be effective only if their implementers are allowed to be formulators because it is people way down in the hierarchy who are in touch with the situation at hand and have the requisite technical expertise. In a sense, these are organizations peopled with craftsmen, all of whom must be strategists.

The conventional view of strategic management, especially in the planning literature, claims that change must be continuous: the organization should be adapting all the time. Yet this view proves to be ironic because the very concept of strategy is rooted in stability, not change. As this same literature makes clear, organizations pursue strategies to set direction, to lay out courses of action, and to elicit cooperation from their members around common, established guidelines. By any definition, strategy imposes stability on an organization. No stability means no strategy (no course to the future, no pattern from the past). Indeed, the very fact of having a strategy, and especially of making it explicit (as the conventional literature implores managers to do), creates resistance to strategic change!

What the conventional view fails to come to grips with, then, is how and when to promote change. A fundamental dilemma of strategy-making is the need to reconcile the forces for stability and for change—to focus efforts and gain operating efficiencies on the one hand, yet adapt and maintain currency with a changing external environment on the other.

QUANTUM LEAPS

Our own research and that of colleagues suggest that organizations resolve these opposing forces by attending first to one and then to the other. Clear periods of stability and change can usually be distinguished in any organization. While it is true that particular strategies may always be changing marginally, it seems equally true that major shifts in strategic orientation occur only rarely.

In our study of Steinberg Inc., a large Quebec supermarket chain headquartered in Montreal, we found only two important reorientations in the 60 years from its founding to the mid-1970s: a shift to self-service in 1933 and the introduction of shopping centers and public financing in 1953. At Volkswagenwerk, we saw only one between the late 1940s and the 1970s, the tumultuous shift from the traditional Beetle to the Audi-type design mentioned earlier. And at Air Canada, we found none over the airline's first four decades, following its initial positioning.

Our colleagues at McGill, Danny Miller and Peter Friesen, found this pattern of change so common in their studies of large numbers of companies (especially the high-performance ones) that they built a theory around it, which they labeled the quantum theory of strategic change (Miller and Friesen, 1984). Their basic point is that organizations adopt two distinctly different modes of behavior at different times.

Most of the time they pursue a given strategic orientation. Change may seem continuous, but it occurs in the context of that orientation (perfecting a given retailing formula, for example) and usually amounts to doing more of the same, perhaps better as well. Most organizations favor these periods of stability because they achieve success not by changing strategies but by exploiting the ones they have. They, like craftsmen, seek continuous improvement by using their distinctive competencies in established courses.

While this goes on, however, the world continues to change, sometimes slowly, occasionally in dramatic shifts. Thus gradually or suddenly, the organization's strategic orientation moves out of sync with its environment. Then, what Miller and Friesen call a strategic revolution must take place. That long period of evolutionary change is suddenly punctuated by a brief bout of revolutionary turmoil in which the organization quickly alters many of its established patterns. In effect, it tries to leap to a new stability quickly to reestablish an integrated posture among a new set of strategies, structures, and culture.

But what about all those emergent strategies, growing like weeds around the organization? What the quantum theory suggests is that the really novel ones are generally held in check in some corner of the organization until a strategic revolution becomes necessary. Then as an alternative to having to develop new strategies from scratch or having to import generic strategies from competitors, the organization can turn to its own emerging patterns to find its new orientation. As the old, established strategy disintegrates, the seeds of the new one begin to spread.

This quantum theory of change seems to apply particularly well to large, established, mass-production companies. Because they are especially reliant on standardized procedures, their resistance to strategic reorientation tends to be especially fierce. So we find long periods of stability broken by short disruptive periods of revolutionary change.

Volkswagenwerk is a case in point. Long enamored of the Beetle and armed with a tightly integrated set of strategies, the company ignored fundamental changes in its markets throughout the late 1950s and 1960s. The bureaucratic momentum of its mass production organization combined with the psychological momentum of its leader, who institutionalized the strategies in the first place. When change finally did come, it was tumultuous; the company groped its way through a hodgepodge of products before it settled on a new set of vehicles championed by a new leader. Strategic reorientations really are cultural revolutions.

CYCLES OF CHANGE

In more creative organizations, we see a somewhat different pattern of change and stability, one that's more balanced. Companies in the business of producing novel outputs apparently need to fly off in all directions from time to time to sustain their creativity. Yet they also need to settle down after such periods to find some order in the resulting chaos.

The National Film Board's tendency to move in and out of focus through remarkably balanced periods of convergence and divergence is a case in point. Concentrated production of films to aid the war effort in the 1940s gave way to great divergence after the war as the organization sought a new raison d'etre. Then the advent of television brought back a very sharp focus in the early 1950s, as noted earlier. But in the late 1950s, this dissipated almost as quickly as it began, giving rise to another creative period of exploration. Then, the social changes in the early 1960s evoked a new period of convergence around experimental films and social issues.

We use the label "adhocracy"* for organizations, like the National Film Board, that produce individual, or custom-made, products (or designs) in an innovative way, on a project basis (Mintzberg, 1981; Mintzberg, 1983). Our craftsman is an adhocracy of sorts too, since each of her ceramic sculptures is unique. And her pattern of strategic change was much like that of the NFB's, with evident cycles of convergence and divergence: a focus on knickknacks from 1967 to 1972; then a period of exploration to about 1976, which resulted in a refocus on ceramic sculptures; that continued to about 1981, to be followed by a period of searching for new directions. More recently, a focus on ceramic murals seems to be emerging.

Whether through quantum revolutions or cycles of convergence and divergence, however, organizations seem to need to separate in time the basic forces for change and stability, reconciling them by attending to each in turn. Many strategic failures can be attributed either to mixing the two or to an obsession with one of these forces at the expense of the other.

The problems are evident in the work of many craftsmen. On the one hand, there are those who seize on the perfection of a single theme and never change. Eventually, the creativity disappears from their work and the world passes them by—much as it did Volkswagenwerk until the company was shocked into its strategic revolution. And then there are those who are always changing, who flit

---

* The term "adhocracy" was coined by Warren G. Bennis and Philip E. Slater in *The Temporary Society* (New York: Harper & Row, 1964).

from one idea to another and never settle down. Because no theme or strategy ever emerges in their work, they cannot exploit or even develop any distinctive competence. And because their work lacks definition, identity crises are likely to develop, with neither the craftsmen nor their clientele knowing what to make of it. Miller and Friesen found this behavior in conventional business too; they label it "the impulsive firm running blind" (Miller and Friesen, 1978). How often have we seen it in companies that go on acquisition sprees?

The popular view sees the strategist as a planner or as a visionary, someone sitting on a pedestal dictating brilliant strategies for everyone else to implement. While recognizing the importance of thinking ahead and especially of the need for creative vision in this pedantic world, I wish to propose an additional view of the strategist—as a pattern recognizer, a learner if you will—who manages a process in which strategies (and visions) can emerge as well as be deliberately conceived. I also wish to redefine that strategist, to extend that someone into the collective entity made up of the many actors whose interplay speaks an organization's mind. This strategist *finds* strategies no less than creates them, often in patterns that form inadvertently in its own behavior.

What, then, does it mean to craft strategy? Let us return to the words associated with craft: dedication, experience, involvement with the material, the personal touch, mastery of detail, a sense of harmony, and integration. Managers who craft strategy do not spend much time in executive suites reading MIS reports or industry analyses. They are involved, responsive to their materials, learning about their organizations and industries through personal touch. They are also sensitive to experience, recognizing that while individual vision may be important, other factors must help determine strategy as well.

Manage Stability

Managing strategy is mostly managing stability, not change. Indeed, most of the time senior managers should not be formulating strategy at all; they should be getting on with making their organizations as effective as possible in pursuing the strategies they already have. Like distinguished craftsmen, organizations become distinguished because they master the details.

To manage strategy, then, at least in the first instance, is not so much to promote change as to know *when* to do so. Advocates of strategic planning often urge managers to plan for perpetual instability in the environment (for example, by rolling over five-year plans annually). But this obsession with change is dysfunctional. Organizations that reassess their strategies continuously are like individuals who reassess their jobs or their marriages continuously—in both cases, people will drive themselves crazy or else reduce themselves to inaction. The formal planning process repeats itself so often and so mechanically that it desensitizes the organization to real change, programs it more and more deeply into set patterns, and thereby encourages it to make only minor adaptations.

So-called strategic planning must be recognized for what it is: a means, not to create strategy, but to program a strategy already created—to work out its implications formally. It is essentially analytic in nature, based on decomposition, while strategy creation is essentially a process of synthesis. That is why trying to create strategies through formal planning most often leads to extrapolating existing ones or copying those of competitors.

This is not to say that planners have no role to play in strategy formation. In addition to programming strategies created by other means, they can feed ad hoc analyses into the strategy-making process at the front end to be sure that the hard data are taken into consideration. They can also stimulate others to think strategically. And of course, people called planners can be strategists too, so long as they are creative thinkers who are in touch with what is relevant. But that has nothing to do with the technology of formal planning.

DETECT DISCONTINUITY

Environments do not change on any regular or orderly basis. And they seldom undergo continuous dramatic change, claims about our "age of discontinuity" and environmental "turbulence" notwithstanding. (Go tell people who lived through the Great Depression or survivors of the siege of Leningrad during World War II that ours are turbulent times.) Much of the time, change is minor and even temporary and requires no strategic response. Once in a while there is a truly significant discontinuity or, even less often, a gestalt shift in the environment, where everything important seems to change at once. But these events, while critical, are also easy to recognize.

The real challenge in crafting strategy lies in detecting the subtle discontinuities that may undermine a business in the future. And for that, there is no technique, no program, just a sharp mind in touch with the situation. Such discontinuities are unexpected and irregular, essentially unprecedented. They can be dealt with only by minds that are attuned to existing patterns yet able to perceive important breaks in them. Unfortunately, this form of strategic thinking tends to atrophy during the long periods of stability that most organizations experience (just as it did at Volkswagenwerk during the 1950s and 1960s). So the trick is to manage within a given strategic orientation most of the time yet be able to pick out the occasional discontinuity that really matters.

The Steinberg chain was built and run for more than half a century by a man named Sam Steinberg. For 20 years, the company concentrated on perfecting a self-service retailing formula introduced in 1933. Installing fluorescent lighting and figuring out how to package meat in cellophane wrapping were the "strategic" issues of the day. Then in 1952, with the arrival of the first shopping center in Montreal, Steinberg realized he had to redefine his business almost overnight. He knew he needed to control those shopping centers and that control would require public financing and other major changes. So he reoriented his business. The ability to make that kind of switch in thinking is the essence of strategic management. And it has more to do with vision and involvement than it does with analytic technique.

KNOW THE BUSINESS

Sam Steinberg was the epitome of the entrepreneur, a man intimately involved with all the details of his business, who spent Saturday mornings visiting his stores. As he told us in discussing his company's competitive advantage:

> Nobody knew the grocery business like we did. Everything has to do with your knowledge. I knew merchandise, I knew cost, I knew selling, I knew customers. I knew everything, and I passed on all my knowledge; I kept teaching my people. That's the advantage we had. Our competitors couldn't touch us.

Note the kind of knowledge involved: not intellectual knowledge, not analytical reports or abstracted facts and figures (though these can certainly help), but personal knowledge, intimate understanding, equivalent to the craftsman's feel for the clay. Facts are available to anyone; this kind of knowledge is not. Wisdom is the word that captures it best. But wisdom is a word that has been lost in the bureaucracies we have built for ourselves, systems designed to distance leaders from operating details. Show me managers who think they can rely on formal planning to create their strategies, and I'll show you managers who lack intimate knowledge of their businesses or the creativity to do something with it.

Craftsmen have to train themselves to see, to pick up things other people miss. The same holds true for managers of strategy. It is those with a kind of peripheral vision who are best able to detect and take advantage of events as they unfold.

MANAGE PATTERNS

Whether in an executive suite in Manhattan or a pottery studio in Montreal, a key to managing strategy is the ability to detect emerging patterns and help them take shape. The job of the manager is not just to preconceive specific strategies but also to recognize their emergence elsewhere in the organization and intervene when appropriate.

Like weeds that appear unexpectedly in a garden, some emergent strategies may need to be uprooted immediately. But management cannot be too quick to cut off the unexpected, for tomorrow's vision may grow out of today's aberration. (Europeans, after all, enjoy salads made from the leaves of the dandelion, America's most notorious weed.) Thus, some patterns are worth watching until their effects have more clearly manifested themselves. Then those that prove useful can be made deliberate and be incorporated into the formal strategy, even if that means shifting the strategic umbrella to cover them.

To manage in this context, then, is to create the climate within which a wide variety of strategies can grow. In more complex organizations, this may mean building flexible structures, hiring creative people, defining broad umbrella strategies, and watching for the patterns that emerge.

RECONCILE CHANGE AND CONTINUITY

Finally, managers considering radical departures need to keep the quantum theory of change in mind. As Ecclesiastes reminds us, there is a time to sow and a time to reap. Some new patterns must be held in check until the organization is ready for a strategic revolution, or at least a period of divergence. Managers who are obsessed with either change or stability are bound eventually to harm their organizations. As pattern recognizer, the manager has to be able to sense when to exploit an established crop of strategies and when to encourage new strains to displace the old.

While strategy is a word that is usually associated with the future, its link to the past is no less central. As Kierkegaard once observed, life is lived forward but understood backward. Managers may have to live strategy in the future, but they must understand it through the past.

Like potters at the wheel, organizations must make sense of the past if they hope to manage the future. Only by coming to understand the patterns that form in their own behavior do they get to know their capabilities and their potential. Thus crafting strategy, like managing craft, requires a natural synthesis of the future, present, and past.

REFERENCES

Miller, D. and Friesen, P.H. (1984). *Organizations: A Quantum View.* Englewood Cliffs, NJ: Prentice-Hall.

Miller, D. and Friesen, P.H. (1978). "Archetypes of Strategy Formulation," *Management Science*, May: 921.

Mintzberg, H. (1981). "Organization Design: Fashion or Fit?" *HBR*, January-February: 103.

Mintzberg, H. (1983). *Structure in Fives: Designing Effective Organizations.* Englewood Cliffs, NJ: Prentice-Hall.

Pascale, R.T., "Perspective on Strategy: The Real Story Behind Honda's Success," *California Management Review*, May-June 1984: 47.

Quinn, J.B. (1988). "IBM (A) Case," in Quinn, J.B., Mintzberg, H., and James, R.M., *The Strategy Process: Concepts, Contexts, Cases.* Englewood Cliffs, NJ: Prentice-Hall.

STRATEGIC DECISIONS AND ALL THAT JAZZ

KATHLEEN M. EISENHARDT

For the past thirty years, research on strategic decisions has been dominated by three basic approaches: "bounded rationality", "power and politics", and "the garbage can".

BOUNDED RATIONALITY In this approach, strategic decision makers are rational, but only within the limits of their own capabilities. They aim for an outcome which is "good enough", rather than the best; they rarely explore options comprehensively; and they often redefine their goals during the process of choosing. While many decisions follow a basic structure of identifying the problem, developing alternatives, analysing and choosing, they also repeat the various stages following different routes.

Bounded rationality is a better description of how people choose than its idealised predecessor, the rational actor model. However, it does not deal well with the fact that many successful decision makers rely heavily on a process that is rational in some ways but not others. For example, effective executives often rationally make contingency plans, but then act on incomplete information; they rationally develop many alternatives, but—apparently not so rationally—fail to analyze them fully. The "bounded rationality" approach says nothing about processes such as insight and intuition, which in reality are likely to be among the most decisive factors in strategic choice.

POWER AND POLITICS The genesis of this model of strategic choice is the political science literature of the 1950s. Like bounded rationality, this perspective is largely a reaction to the rational actor model. In this case, the particular feature under attack is the assumption that organizations have a single goal, ordained from on high. So, while bounded rationality attacks the model of the individual as rational, the political model attacks the model of the group as rational. In the political model, people are individually rational, but not collectively so. Choice is the outcome of a process in which conflict among decision makers is resolved through the use of politics and power.

Most would agree that organizations consist of people who have partially conflicting preferences surrounding their individual and collective self-interest. It is also common ground that strategic choice processes are invariably political in that powerful people usually get what they want, and that people use political tactics like coalition formation, withholding information, and lobbying to enhance their power and point of view.

Reprinted by permission of Blackwell Publishing Ltd. From "Strategic Decisions and All That Jazz," by Kathleen Eisenhardt, *Business Strategy Review*, Autumn 1997:8:3:1(3).

However, the "power and politics" approach can assume too much rationality and deviousness. Like "bounded rationality", it neglects the emotional aspect of choice. Power and politics often involve emotions such as animosity and jealousy, which are not part of the paradigm. The traditional paradigm lacks a soul.

THE GARBAGE CAN The garbage can model emphasizes the role of chance in the unfolding of strategic decisions. Decision-making occurs through the random meeting of choices looking for problems, decision makers looking for something to decide, problems looking for solutions, and so forth.

Empirical research suggests that chance does play a major role in decision making. Moreover, the "garbage can" perspective is particularly relevant as the time frame of choice stretches out, deadlines are removed and where organizations more closely resemble organized anarchy.

Yet, for decision makers in real corporations, the garbage can model is seductive but frustrating. Beyond the importance of timing, it has little to say that is normative: about how to improve the decision-making process. Yet, this is precisely the problem that real decision makers face.

TOWARDS A NEW MODEL: IMPROVISATION

For real strategic decision makers, decisions require quality. They may not be the "best", but they have to be at least "good enough". In today's corporate context, competition is just too severe to allow for poor strategic choices. Today's corporate context demands fast decisions that are flexible enough to permit adaptation as circumstances change. There is tension between deciding quickly and adaptively in the context of rapid change while at the same time executing on time and on budget in the context of punishing competition.

There are doubtless many possible metaphors for thinking about this dilemma. The particular one that I outline here is improvisation. Improvisation is often discussed in the context of the arts: jazz improvisation such as that by Dave Brubeck and Miles Davis, rock improvisation by bands such as the Grateful Dead and Pearl Jam, and dramatic improvisation in movies such as *Secrets and Lies* or by troupes like Chicago's Second City. Recently, improvisation has made its way into discussions of organizational processes, notably in product development.

What is improvisation? It is organizing in such a way that the actors both adaptively innovate and efficiently execute. In music, this means creating good music in real time, while constantly adjusting to the shifting musical interpretations of other group members.

The popular conception of improvisation is that the actors or musicians are simply performing whatever takes their fancy at that moment. But, in reality, true improvisation is much more structured. It is distinguished by two very crucial characteristics.

■ First, improvisation relies upon performers intensely communicating with each other in real time. In musical improvisation, this means constantly paying attention to whatever the musicians who are playing at the moment are doing. Effective improvisation requires performers neither to look back at what has been played already nor to glance ahead to when they may cut in. They play very much in the "now".

- Second, improvisation involves performers relying on a few, very specific rules. There are not many rules, but those that do exist are religiously followed. Improvisational bands typically have a few rules around the order of play and the acceptable chords. But, beyond these, the musicians are free to play as they choose.

The result of improvisation is a performance that is innovative, surprising and adaptive while, in the hands of skilled performers, it is also high quality and well-executed. Improvisation produces music that is more spontaneous and adaptive than, for example, classical symphonies, but also more melodious and indeed "musical" than simply random play.

Why does improvisation produce adaptive yet well-executed performance? The limited rules provide an overarching framework such that even musicians who have never played together before can still create good music. Without such structure, there are too many degrees of freedom. Yet, at the same time, there is not so much structure that the adaptability and innovativeness of the performance is restricted. Further, the real-time attention and interaction keep performers centered on working together to continuously balance flexibility and execution.

This same kind of adaptive, yet efficient performance is critical for effective strategic decision making, especially in fast-changing and highly competitive settings. In particular, an improvisational view assumes that strategic choice is conducted by a small group of decision makers. Like musicians, these executives are skilled individuals, often with a particular expertise. However, instead of expertise with particular musical instruments and music forms, their expertise centers on functional areas such as finance or geographic location, or some other source of expertise. Moreover, while these decision makers are individuals, their task is collective: to make effective strategic choices that blend adaptiveness and execution.

The idea that a jazz band is a useful metaphor for strategic decision making is, I think, unexplored. Nonetheless, in my research with Jay Bourgeois and Jeannie Kahwajy, the improvisational model seems to unify and explain the results that we obtained. This research consists of in-depth case studies of strategic decision making among the top management teams of 12 computer firms. The most effective decision makers relied on limited structure in their strategic decision processes. In particular, they insisted upon a large number of alternatives and the use of conflict-generating processes of investigation—like multiple scenarios—to create and explore these alternatives. But, they did not specify any particular decision process and they did not extensively analyze most of the alternatives.

These decision makers also relied heavily on roles. Much like having musicians with particular instruments, these top managers took on specific roles such as counsellor, devil's advocate, Mr. Steady, Ms. Action, and guru. But precisely what decision makers did in the context of these roles was not specified. The more effective decision makers also relied on a process for resolving conflict termed "consensus with qualification". This means that the group tries to reach consensus;

but, if that consensus is not achieved, then the choice falls to a particular group member (e.g., the CEO or head of a function) (Eisenhardt et al, 1997a, b, c). Again, the process had some structure, but it was not entirely rigid; team members could probe for consensual decisions, yet still had a way to make the choice in the absence of such consensus.

We also observed in these effective teams that the strategic decision-makers, like jazz musicians, paid close attention to real time. Compared with less effective top management teams, they had an unusually high amount of communication, both formal and informal, with one another. They also had an intense focus on real-time information about their businesses. They had an unusually tight grip on a small number of operating variables. They did not look to the past very much, and they did not spend much time looking ahead very far either. They were very much in the "now".

The implications of our research are that these top management teams achieved a number of positive outcomes with their approach to decision making that are consistent with improvisation. Their decisions were typically fast and adaptive to environmental change, high quality because they were the result of conflict-based discussion, and achieved broad acceptance because of the group involvement. Overall, although these results are not definitive, they do suggest that an improvisational model may provide fresh insights into effective strategic choice, especially in fast-changing and highly competitive settings.

REFERENCES

Brown, S.L. and Eisenhardt, K.M. (1998). *Competing on the Edge: Strategy as Structured Chaos*, Cambridge, MA: Harvard Business School Press.

Eisenhardt, K.M. (1990a). "Speed and Strategic Choice," *California Management Review*, 32:3, 39–54.

Eisenhardt, K.M. and Bourgeois III, L.J. (1990b). "Charting Strategic Decisions in the Microcomputer Industry: Profile of an Industry Star," in M. von Glinow and S. Mohrman (eds.), *Managing Complexity in High Technology Organizations*, Oxford University Press.

Eisenhardt, K.M., Kahwajy, J.L. and Bourgeois III, L.J. (1997a). "Taming Interpersonal Conflict in Strategic Choice: How Top Management Teams Argue but Still Get Along," in V. Papadakis and P. Barwise (eds.), *Strategic Decisions*, Boston: Kluwer Academic Publishers.

Eisenhardt, K.M., Kahwajy, J.L. and Bourgeois III, L.J. (1997b). "Conflict and Strategic Choice: How Top Management Teams Disagree," *California Management Review*, 39:2, 42–62.

Eisenhardt, K.M., Kahwajy, J.L. and Bourgeois III, L.J. (1997c). "How Teams Have a Good Fight," *Harvard Business Review*, July-August.

QUESTIONS: SECTION FOUR

THE ORIGIN OF STRATEGY
BRUCE D. HENDERSON

1. What distinction does Henderson make between Darwinian natural selection and strategy?

2. How are business competition and biological competition *similar*?

3. How does Henderson suggest a company can grow and prosper?

4. How do "natural competition" and "strategic commitment" differ?

5. Are, as Henderson argues, biologists better guides to business than economists?

CRAFTING STRATEGY
HENRY MINTZBERG

1. What are the differences between "planning" and "crafting"? Why does Mintzberg think crafting describes effective business strategy better than planning?

2. How does pottery-making give insight into linking strategy formulation and implementation?

3. Describe the continuum of strategy: from deliberate to emergent. Where does "crafting" belong on this continuum? How do potters use this continuum when practicing their craft? How can a business strategist use the continuum? How can business strategists achieve "deliberate emergence," in which they operate in between the two extremes of the continuum?

4. How can periods of convergence and divergence be effectively managed?

5. Why does Mintzberg recommend that strategists focus on managing *stability*, not change?

6. What attributes and abilities do successful craftsmen have that business strategists also need?

STRATEGIC DECISIONS AND ALL THAT JAZZ
KATHLEEN EISENHARDT

1. Eisenhardt briefly discusses the approaches to strategy of "bounded rationality," "power and politics," and "the garbage can." What does she find lacking in each of these approaches?

2. What is the structure of jazz improvisation?

3. What musical benefits does improvisation yield? How is an improvisa-tional approach to business strategy superior to the models of strategy dis-cussed previously?

4. Are there companies and/or environmental conditions in which improvi-sational strategy is more appropriate than others? Where might improvis-ing *not* be the best approach?

5

ENDLESS JOURNEY

Berkshire is my painting, so it should look the way I want it to when it's done.

—Warren Buffet (from Bianco, 1999)

Take comfort if you find yourself perplexed at the sight of artist Jackson Pollock's murals. As an abstract expressionist Pollock was not concerned that his paintings have literal meaning to the viewer. He preferred to express himself more in the *process* of his painting versus the output. When we see his work, we are to imagine him striding around his often huge canvases towing cans of paint. And instead of brushes we should envision him using cruder tools—sticks, trowels, and the like. The result is hard to define, as Pollock wanted it.

> When I am in my painting, I'm not aware of what I'm doing. It's only after a sort of 'get acquainted' period that I see what I have been about. I have no fears about making changes, destroying the image, etc., because the painting has a life of its own. I try to let it come through. (Jackson Pollock, 1947)

Many of the works that employed Pollock's trademark drip method appear irrational and chaotic. They are as open to the viewer's imagination as a Rorschach inkblot; and like a Rorschach, their interpretation says more about the viewer than about the work itself. Pollock gives us little guidance, scant direction. The even treatment across his works gives the impression that being in one location on the canvas is very much like being in any other part of it. We sense there are no boundaries to his paintings; that if we were to step outside them, we would find more of the same erratic pattern, on and on.

The painting style of photo-realism, on the other hand, seems more accessible, at least on the surface. Artists like Richard Estes gained recognition in the 1960s for an exaggerated attention to detail that made common sites like storefronts or diners appear to be photographs. One can only imagine the tedious brushwork that is required of the artist; the level of precision and control needed in applying paint to canvas. The result is often hyper-realistic. In striking contrast to Pollock's abstract expressionism, the photo-realist clearly defines the boundaries of the scene and essentially confines our interpretation of it. In fact, the works seem to pull the viewer so magnetically into the specifics that it is easy to forget what the painting represents. This is the irony. How much more realistic and representational could an artist hope to become?

Stand very close to a canvas by the French impressionist Claude Monet: perhaps one of his signature water lily paintings. What you'll see appears to be the surface of a rock, or maybe a Landsat photograph. Surprisingly, it might even remind you of Pollock's mural. Step back, however, and you'll see more of what Monet had in mind. The impressionists are credited with popularizing the *plein aire* technique in painting, working not in a studio, but outside in the immediacy of the artist's subject. Monet and his fellow impressionists were considered heretics when their novel style was introduced in the late 1800s. Art connoisseurs were unaccustomed to a style in which subjects, although recognizable, were blurred, their detail softened. Up close, the artist's broad-brush strokes, often rendered in thick oils, look crude and unrefined. Colors were placed on the canvas unmixed. And, yet, when viewed from a distance, the impressionists' brilliance in capturing the vagaries of light on their subjects becomes undeniable. Monet used landscapes, haystacks, and cathedrals as his vehicles for expressing light. In his later years, he focused his painting on his garden in Giverny, France. The garden still lives; but never quite in the way Monet rendered it in his paintings.

How are impressionism, abstract expressionism, and photo-realism related to business strategy? In Monet's approach the strategist's framework provides a sense of direction, but in a manner that leaves room to maneuver. Close to the "canvas" our actions can go a variety of ways and appear even random. But step back and these actions take on a recognizable form. Jackson Pollock drops us into an incoherent world without any boundaries on thought or action. With Pollock there is no moving forward, and no moving back. We rely on purely subjective interpretation of an unintelligible creation. No strategy here. Photo-realism, in contrast, gives us a very clear sense of direction, but its approach to strategy binds us to a single interpretation of the future. We are stifled, hemmed in by what we believe to be real and unmalleable. What we gain in precision, we lose in accuracy.

The strategic thinking necessary to take an organization forward lies somewhere in between Pollock's chaos and the nauseating detail of photo-realism. Monet's approach is the bridge. His strategic impressionism provides enough structure to guide, but not so much as to stifle and confine. Boundaries on thinking exist, but are dotted lines. "In strategy," writes 17th-century samurai Miyamoto Musashi in his *Book of Five Rings*, "it is important to see distant things as if they were close and to take a distanced view of close things." Monet is the master of strategic thinking.

■ ■ ■

The readings in this book share a common theme: strategic thinking requires the variegated set of lenses that metaphors provide. Where football doesn't work, evolutionary biology may—or Sun Tzu, musical improvisation, even fine art. While metaphor is particularly useful in periods of great change that require radically new visions, metaphors from history—even ancient history—continue to offer a rich pallet of ideas for strategists.

The journey does not end here, however. The challenges of navigating modern business will surely demand that we continually reach out of context to unearth—and to create—an even more powerful portfolio of metaphors in the future.

QUESTIONS: SECTION FIVE

1. What metaphors beyond those covered in *Out of Context* would spur creative thinking in business strategy?

2. What metaphor or metaphors would best depict your approach to strategic management?

3. What influences do you think have contributed to your approach?

4. How would your approach enhance—or perhaps limit—your ability to conceive of a future direction and communicate it to others?

References

Akin, G. and Palmer, I. (2000). "Putting Metaphors to Work for Change in Organizations." *Organizational Dynamics*. Winter: 67–79.

Bianco, A. (1999). "The Warren Buffet You Don't Know." *Businessweek*. July 5: 55–66.

Braley, B. (1917). "Business Is Business." Originally published in Braley's *A Banjo at Armageddon*, George H. Doran Company, NY. More recently published in *Virtues in Verse: The Best of Berton Braley* (Vol. 1), selected and arranged by Linda Tania Abrams, The Atlantean Press, 1993.

Brooks, C. and Warren, R.P. (1970). "Metaphor." *Modern Rhetoric, Third Edition*. New York: Harcourt, Brace and World, Inc.: 436.

Edwards, O. (2001). "Villain Grace High Tech Heroes Are a Dime a Dozen." *Forbes*. May 28.

Forbes, ASAP (2000). "It's Like, the Truth Can Be Elusive—An Interview with Scott McNealy," 10/02.

Glucksberg, S., Manfredi, D.A. and McGlone, M.S. (1997). "Metaphor Comprehension: How Metaphors Create New Categories." Ward, T.B. et al (eds.), *Creative Thought: An Investigation of Conceptual Structures and Processes*, Washington, D.C.: American Psychological Association: 327–328.

Goett, P. (2002). "The Puck Stops Here." *Journal of Business Strategy*. 21(6): 2.

Hamm, S. (2000). "Oracle—Why It's Cool Again." *Businessweek*. May 8: 114.

Kao, John J. (1997). "The Art and Discipline of Business Creativity." *Strategy and Leadership*, July/August: 6–11.

Katz, R.L. (1954). "Executive Skills: What Makes a Good Administrator?" in C.C. Lundberg, "Management Development Revisited." *Personnel Administration*, Vol. 29 (Jan-Feb, 1966): 39–44.

Lakoff, G. and Johnson, M. (1980). *Metaphors We Live By.* Chicago: University of Chicago Press.

Mintzberg, H. (1994). "The Fall and Rise of Strategic Planning." *Harvard Business Review.* January-February: 109.

Musashi, M. *Book of Five Rings.* Translated by Victor Harris (1974). Woodstock, NY: The Overlook Press.

Pollock, J. (1947-48). "My Painting." *Possibilities* (New York) #1. Winter: 79.

Ward, T.B., Smith, S.M., and Vaid, J. (eds.). *Creative Thought: An Investigation of Conceptual Structures and Processes.* Washington, D.C.: American Psychological Association: 14.